JUSTIN WILSON
LOOKING BACK

How y'all are? Me, I'm casting mah eye back (maybe you would say looking back) and me, I'm having mah enjoys seeing wat I see: Cookin' de good foods and de wondermous Cajun frien's that I had and still got, I garontee!
(Photo by Lamar D. Tuminello)

JUSTIN WILSON
LOOKING BACK
A Cajun Cookbook

PELICAN PUBLISHING COMPANY
Gretna 1997

*The word "Pelican" and the depiction of a pelican are trademarks
of Pelican Publishing Company, Inc., and are registered in the
U.S. Patent and Trademark Office.*

Library of Congress Cataloging-in-Publication Data

Wilson, Justin.
    Justin Wilson looking back : a Cajun cookbook ; [photographs by
    David King Gleason].
          p.   cm.
    Includes index.
    ISBN 1-56554-282-7 (alk. paper)
    1. Cookery, American—Louisiana style. 2. Cookery, Cajun.
    I. Title. II. Title: Looking back.
    TX715.2.L68W57 1997
641.59763—dc21   97-9757
                                                      CIP

Photographs by David King Gleason and Bill Cooksey

Sarah Sue Goldsmith, consulting editor

Manufactured in the United States of America

Published by Pelican Publishing Company, Inc.
1101 Monroe Street, Gretna, Louisiana 70053

To my late wife Sara,
who was a damn good cook, too, I garontee!

Sara an' me, we took some time out from cookin' to see if maybe the drinkin' wine done gone bad or somethin'. (Photo by Bill Cooksey)

Contents

Le's see, now. Was that one cup wine an' four clove garlic, or four cup wine an' one clove garlic? (Photo by Bill Cooksey)

Preface

Me, I'm in love!

With cookin', that is, in case my girl friends is readin' this.

An' I done got me this love affair more years behind than I like to confess, although I an't nearly so ol' as some peoples think I is!

Mos' especially, I'm in love with cookin' Cajun-style, since I done brought myself up among these wondermous people, the Louisiana Cajuns.

What I love mos' about Cajun cookin' is the imagines what they done put into it.

You see, my frien', although some Cajuns is rich as thick cream, mos' of them Cajuns ain't got the money to buy them fancy cuts of meat and high price' vegetables. An' that's where the imagines comes in.

Down through the centuries, the Louisiana Cajun, like his French cousin, has learned to improvise, usin' the less expensive meats an' vegetables in they cookin'.

There is certain—how you call it—staples what the Cajun cooks with mos' ever' day of his life. Stuff like rice, cornmeal, red beans, peas, okra, tomatoes, an' eggplant.

Cajuns cook a lot of chicken, pork, cheap cuts of beef, and lamb. An', bein' some of the most greates' hunters in the worl', they also eat lots of rabbit, squirrel, venison, 'coon, an' duck.

But maybe the most bes' things the Cajun cooks is things like shrimp, catfish, crabs, oysters, an' turtle, what he usually catch hisself.

Now, mos' anybody can cook a meal if he can read writin'. An' there is lots of good cookbooks what you can buy.

But this little cookbook is somethin' different. It ain't exactly—how you call it—a "beginner's" book. It ain't gonna tol' you how to boil a egg or cook a steak.

Howsomever, there ain't a recipe in this book that you can't cook—an' good, too—providin' you got the right attitude.

The right attitude is made up from two things: You' imagines and you' common ol' horse sense, which the Cajun has hisself a barrel of. If you looks on cookin' as fun, which it sure can be, you got you'self a runnin' start on becomin' a Cajun cook.

Once you learn to make a fine roux, to boil rice, to make barbecue sauce from scratch, an' to use the seasonin's you find in this book, then cookin' Cajun-style is gonna become fun, I garontee.

An' you gonna use wine in you' cookin'. A little sauterne, or white wine, a little claret, sometimes a little sherry can make a mos' ordinair' dish taste like somethin' cooked by angels.

If you got the prohibits about wine, don' you worry none. The alcohol done cook itse'f right out of that pot in jus' ten or nine seconds. An' all what you got lef' is that wondermous flavor.

But the real basic thing about Cajun cookin' is still imagines an' common sense, I garontee.

You' imagines eventually gonna tell you to add a little somethin' here, a little somethin' there, to these recipes. 'Sperimentin' gonna come easy pretty soon. You' common sense gonna tell you what goes good with what, an' when, too. You gonna know you don't put you' sawmill gravy on them prunes.

So, one of these days, you gonna cast you' eye over somethin' you is cookin' an you gonna realize that you is a good Cajun cook. Maybe not so good like Uncle Justin, but good! An' that day, you gonna discover that you usin' all five of you' senses when you cook.

You' taste sense is the first big one. Then you' smell sense, he come on big. An' you eye sense come along pretty fas' too. Even you' feel sense gonna come in handy, time to time. But one day or so, you gonna caught you'self listenin' to see if you' rice is finish cook or not.

That gonna be the day you gonna yell "Hoo, boy, I finally is a Cajun cook, for sure!"

Me, I done eaten every dish in this little book maybe four or three hundred times. An' it make me sad for you because you been missin' so much all you' life.

When you try Uncle Justin's Cajun dishes, you' gonna have the time of you' life, I garontee!

Bon soir! Bon appetit!

—Justin Wilson, October 1965

Introduction

I was reared on a truck farm between Amite City and Roseland, Louisiana. When I was eight years old, I didn't like to work in the fields. When Mama told Papa she needed help in the kitchen, I volunteered immediately.

Naturally I didn't start cooking immediately, but I watched a great deal, and by osmosis I couldn't help but learn many things.

It was so much fun working with Mama because she had a terrific sense of humor. When I finally did start cooking a little with her, she didn't fuss at me when I made mistakes. She laughed like hell and said, "We're going to have to do that over!" Even as young as I was—at least ten—I realized that I was with one of the greatest creative cooks in the world.

One of the first things I had to do over was to cook okra. Mama told me to get the slime out of it. Most people call it slime. I don't; I call it thick juice. But I cooked it until I burnt it. Then I had no slime, but I also had no okra.

Mama showed me what she meant by taking the slime out. I said, "Mama, there's still slime in this." She said, "Of course there is. That's where the flavor is." From that time on, I had the pleasure of watching my mother create dishes from leftovers and from practically nothing.

Years later, when I was working as a safety engineer—which I still am—and giving talks all over the country, a dear friend, Jack Moler, who was city editor of the *Houston Press* and later the *Houston Chronicle,* got the idea I should write a cookbook.

I would cook for the *Houston Press* and other people. That's how I became friends with Jack. That particular time, I had spent three days cooking on stage for Houston Natural Gas, and Jack said, "Look, you have to write a cookbook." I told him, "You've got to go find your mind because you have lost it!"

But with his help and a lot of trepidation, we wrote a cookbook called *The Justin Wilson Cook Book.* It had 89 pages and was published in 1965. The only way I could write it was I had to cook the stuff. I never measured ingredients so I didn't know how much of anything went into my dishes.

I had to make a flying trip to Houston once because Jack said my

Me, Sara, and my mama. (Photo by David King Gleason)

jambalaya recipe didn't work. I told him to make the recipe while I watched. All that was wrong was he didn't have enough water—one cup.

That cookbook was among the first Cajun cookbooks. We published it ourselves and got a wonderful response. We sold 5,000 copies in about a month. The price was $2.95. In 1979, I put together *The Justin Wilson #2 Cookbook: Cookin' Cajun.* Both of those early cookbooks are combined here; that's why I call it *Justin Wilson Looking Back: A Cajun Cookbook.*

People always ask me how I got a cooking show on television. This is how it happened:

I was sitting in a little restaurant in Denham Springs, Louisiana, right outside of Baton Rouge, when a young man walked up to me and said, "Mr. Wilson, my name is Bob Rowland. I am with Mississippi ETV."

I said, "Bob, that doesn't spell a damn thing."

He said, "No, but it stands for Mississippi Educational Television and we would like for you to do a cooking show for us."

That was 1971. I told him, "You must be crazy to think I can cook on television." He said, "I might be, but I believe we could have a good show." And I hope we did. It had to be the first Cajun cooking show on television, but it was seen only by people in that area.

Looking back, there's very little difference in the cooking style, but you learn certain things as you go along, and you make small changes to improve the recipes. For instance, certain seasonings are overpowering—like celery. I use less celery now and more parsley. And instead of bay leaves, I changed over to dried mint. I use more olive oil now, instead of oleo.

When we cooked back then, we used sauterne wine because it was white and dry and took out the bitterness of seasonings like celery, bell pepper, parsley, onions, and green onions. Since it's hard to find sauterne now, I use chablis. I won't use a wine I would not or could not drink.

I remember that Mama ate those little bird's-eye peppers like they were popcorn, but she taught me that food should be well seasoned and tasty—not hot, hot, hot.

Many of the recipes in this book are things Mama taught me. I am happy to share them all with you, along with some of my memories, looking back . . .

—Justin Wilson, July 4, 1996

ABBREVIATIONS

STANDARD			METRIC		
tsp.	=	teaspoon	ml.	=	milliliter
tbsp.	=	tablespoon	l.	=	liter
oz.	=	ounce	g.	=	gram
qt.	=	quart	kg.	=	kilogram
lb.	=	pound	mg.	=	milligram

STANDARD-METRIC APPROXIMATIONS

⅛ teaspoon	=	.6 milliliter			
¼ teaspoon	=	1.2 milliliters			
½ teaspoon	=	2.5 milliliters			
1 teaspoon	=	5 milliliters			
1 tablespoon	=	15 milliliters			
4 tablespoons	=	¼ cup	=	60 milliliters	
8 tablespoons	=	½ cup	=	118 milliliters	
16 tablespoons	=	1 cup	=	236 milliliters	
2 cups	=	473 milliliters			
2½ cups	=	563 milliliters			
4 cups	=	946 milliliters			
1 quart	=	4 cups	=	.94 liter	

SOLID MEASUREMENTS

½ ounce	=	15 grams			
1 ounce	=	25 grams			
4 ounces	=	110 grams			
16 ounces	=	1 pound	=	454 grams	

JUSTIN WILSON
LOOKING BACK

I wanna let you know rat now dat I'm very saincaire about dis cookin' business. I believe it when I say cookin' is not'ing but imagination an' common sense in the proper amounts. (Photo by David King Gleason)

HOW TO MAKE A ROUX

Ooh, boy! Dat's a relief, I garontee! It came out jus' like I t'ought it would. But I had my own doubts dare for a little while, you hear? (Photo by David King Gleason)

ROUX

The "roux" is the foundation of many, many Cajun dishes. You will find it referred to in a number of the recipes in this book. The roux that follows is the one I have used for many years, with great success—I garontee!

Olive oil   **1½ cups sifted flour**

Cover the bottom of a heavy pot with olive oil. After the olive oil is well heated over a slow fire, stir in the flour. Cook the flour very slowly, stirring almost constantly. The flour must be browned to a very dark brown, nearly black, but not actually burned.

This takes more time than you might think is necessary, but a good roux must be cooked slowly to get all floury taste out of it and to ensure uniformity of color. This is the basic roux.

Although all roux are pretty much the same in Cajun kitchens, there are variations practiced by some stubborn ol' cooks that I won't attempt to go into here.

However, as you read this book, you'll see where several recipes call for a couple of additional ingredients.

For instance, after you have made the basic roux, you can add a small can of tomato paste, stirring this all the time until the roux has reached the color of the flour before the paste was added. Then add a small can of tomato sauce, stirring this into the mixture until it all turns dark brown again.

Couple ol' Cajuns sometime spend a whole afternoon like this—seein' who can lie the bes'! That's old man Malbrough passin' the time with me.
(Photo by Bill Cooksey)

APPETIZERS AND DIPS

Smell them aromas, you! But don' reach out for that yet, or you gonna draw back a stump. (Photo by Bill Cooksey)

BOILED BURR ARTICHOKES

2-4 fresh young burr
   artichokes
¾ cup olive oil
1 large onion, quartered
¼ cup lemon juice
2 large cloves garlic

3-4 cups claret, Sauterne,
   or dry white wine
Louisiana red hot sauce
1 tbsp. Worcestershire sauce
Water
Salt to taste

Wash artichokes well, and let them drain. Put them in a pot large enough for liquids to cover them, or nearly so. Pour olive oil over them, and put onions, lemon juice, and garlic in the pot. Pour wine over the artichokes, and add Louisiana hot sauce and Worcestershire sauce. Add enough water to cover. Salt to taste.

Cook, covered, over medium flame, adding water as needed. It is not necessary, however, to keep the artichokes covered with liquid when they near completion of cooking.

Cook until outside leaves are very tender. After artichokes are done, keep them covered so they will steam for about 30 minutes. Cool or chill and serve.

Because these are cooked with seasonings, nothing additional is needed for them to taste wonderful, but you can serve them with a lemon-butter sauce if you want to. *Serves 4-8.*

"Serves 4 to 8, depending on how artichoke hungry you are. Hell, I can eat all that myself, when I'm artichoke hungry!

"My papa, the late Harry D. Wilson, he done said one time he jus' as soon eat a pine burr as a artichoke. So nex' time I fix this recipe, he got himse'f a pine burr on his plate.

"An' I ain' gonna tell you what he said 'bout that, 'cause this book paper done burn right up if I do.

"But when he try this recipe, he change his mind, and from then on he fightin' for his burr artichoke, jus' like the rest of us."

This ain' no fancy supermarket. But if you want it an' that Cajun, Aubrey Le Place, ain' got it, he gonna git it for you, for sure. (Photo by Bill Cooksey)

COPPER PENNIES

SAUCE

½ cup salad oil
1 cup sugar
¾ cup vinegar

1 can tomato soup
1 tbsp. dry mustard
1 tbsp. Worcestershire sauce

Simmer in a saucepan the salad oil, sugar, vinegar, tomato soup, mustard, and Worcestershire sauce.

VEGETABLES

2 lb. carrots, sliced
1 medium onion, sliced

1 small green pepper, sliced

Boil the carrots until tender. (Remember, if you use canned carrots, you don't have to cook them!)

In a casserole dish, alternate in layers the carrots, onions, and peppers. Pour sauce over the vegetables and refrigerate until ready to serve. *Serves 8-10.*

"Le' me tol' you the wondermous part about us Cajuns. We don't need no appetizers 'cause we got an appetite soon as we sit down, yeah. I don' even need no cookin' aromas, no. The kind of appetite I got wake up wit' me in the mornin', every mornin'. I tol' you for true!"

Lagniappe: In South Louisiana, "lagniappe" means a little something extra. In the old days, you might buy 100 pounds of rice, and the storekeeper would say, "I threw in candy for the children for lagniappe." Times have changed, and you aren't likely to get something for free at the store today, but people still use the term frequently.

GARLIC BREAD AU BEAUJOLAIS

2 sticks butter, softened
1 tbsp. pressed garlic or garlic
   puree
Grated Romano or Parmesan
   cheese

Black ground pepper
Loaf of French bread
Beaujolais wine

Preheat the oven to 325 degrees.

Mix the softened butter with either pressed garlic or garlic puree to taste. Add to the butter enough grated Romano or Parmesan cheese so that it will still spread easily. Sprinkle with black ground pepper. Slice French bread in half, lengthwise. Spread garlic butter on generously. Toast in oven at 325 degrees until lightly brown.

Dip garlic bread in Beaujolais wine when eating it. This is known as dunking, and you will find that it is delicious. Don't mind the crumbs in your wine—you'll eat those, too. Dunking should be done while eating your meal. *Serves 6.*

"Now some folks say it's bad manners to dunk you' garlic bread in you' wine. An' I mus' admit this is good, even if you bite a big chunk of this bread and chase it with a little wine.

"But me, I like to dunk, an' I don' think dunkin' is bad, neither. An' it taste so good with you' meal, too.

"So don't forgot, it ain't no sin to dunk. An' if it is, who give a dam' anyway?"

TANGY MEATBALLS

1 lb. ground beef
1 egg, slightly beaten
¼ cup chili sauce
¼ cup finely chopped onion

1 tsp. salt
¼ tsp. ground cayenne pepper
1½ cups cheese-cracker crumbs
Cooking oil

Combine the ground beef, egg, chili sauce, chopped onion, salt, and pepper with 1 cup cheese-cracker crumbs. Mix thoroughly. Shape into tiny meatballs, and roll in the remaining ½ cup cracker crumbs.

Sauté the meatballs 5 minutes in ½ inch of hot cooking oil, turning to brown on all sides. Remove to a chafing dish, and serve with toothpicks. *Makes about 30 meatballs.*

SMOKED SAUSAGE AND OYSTERS À LA JUSTIN

2 lb. country smoked sausage
1 qt. medium-sized fresh
   oysters
2 cups Sauterne wine or dry
   white wine

1 tsp. Louisiana hot sauce
½ tsp. garlic salt
½ tsp. salt
Juice from ½ lemon

Cut sausage in 1-inch pieces, and place in large frying pan—preferably an iron one. Add oysters, wine, hot sauce, garlic salt, salt, and lemon juice. Bring to a good boil, then turn fire down so that it will cook slowly.

Cook until most of the juice is gone, leaving just enough to serve as gravy, if you wish. Be sure the sausage is well cooked and tender. This may be served either as an appetizer or as a main dish. *Serves 6-8.*

Louisiana Hot Sauce Marinated Shrimp

3 lb. raw shrimp (fresh or
    frozen)
2 12-oz. bottles (or cans) beer
½ tsp. Justin Wilson's
    Louisiana Hot Sauce
1 tbsp. salt

1 tbsp. dry mustard
2 tbsp. vinegar
1 slice onion
2 tbsp. honey
¼ tsp. bitters (Peychaud or
    Angostura)

Remove shells and veins from shrimp. Rinse.

In a saucepan, combine beer, hot sauce, salt, mustard, vinegar, onion, honey, and bitters. Bring to a boil and simmer about 1 minute.

Add only enough cleaned shrimp as will be covered by the liquid mixture; return the mixture to a boil, and then simmer 2 to 5 minutes, depending on the size of the shrimp.

Remove shrimp from the liquid, add remaining shrimp, and repeat the cooking procedure.

Cool both the shrimp and the liquid. Return the shrimp to the cooled liquid, and marinate for several hours. Drain.

Serve the shrimp with wooden toothpicks as hors d'oeuvres or as an appetizer. *Makes about 24 servings.*

Shrimp Dip

1 8-oz. pkg. soft cream cheese
Juice from 1 lemon
2 lb. boiled shrimp, coarsely
    ground
10 green onions, minced

Mayonnaise
Hot sauce to taste
Worcestershire sauce to taste
Salt and pepper to taste

Soften cream cheese with lemon juice. Add shrimp and green onions to cream cheese mixture. Add enough mayonnaise to give a consistency for dipping potato chips or crackers.

Season with hot sauce, Worcestershire sauce, salt, and pepper.

This is much better if made 8 hours prior to serving time. Add more seasoning if desired. *Serves 10-15.*

HOT SWISS 'N' CIDER DIP

½ lb. Swiss processed cheese,
   diced
1½ tsp. flour
1½ cups sweet apple cider or
   apple juice

½ tsp. salt
⅛ tsp. pepper
¼ tsp. parsley or chives, finely
   chopped
Dash garlic salt

Sprinkle diced cheese with flour.

Heat cider to boiling point, then reduce heat to simmer. Add floured cheese, gradually stirring until all the cheese is melted.

Add seasoning to make a good, zippy dip to be used with French bread wedges or potato chips. *Serves about 15.*

CRAWFISH COCKTAIL

20 to 25 lb. live crawfish
½ cup chili sauce
½ cup catsup
¼ cup horseradish
1½ tsp. Worcestershire sauce

¼ tsp. salt
2 tsp. lemon juice
½ cup finely minced celery
Louisiana hot sauce or
   cayenne pepper sauce

Boil the crawfish in well-salted water about 15 minutes. Mix the rest of the ingredients together for the cocktail sauce.

Fill a large bowl with chopped ice, and arrange crawfish tails over the top. Provide toothpicks for handy dipping.

Serve with the cocktail sauce. *Serves approximately 6-8 people (about 3 lb. of crawfish per person).*

Tasty Black-eyed Pea Dip

½ lb. dried black-eyed peas
Water to cover
1 cup water
1 cup Sauterne wine or dry
    white wine
1¼ tsp. salt
⅓ cup diced lean ham
1 4-oz. can green chiles

½ tsp. red food coloring
1 cup tomato juice
½ cup chopped onion
⅛ tsp. garlic powder
½ jar (8 oz.) processed cheese
    spread
¼ tsp. hot pepper sauce

Wash peas, cover with water, and allow to soak overnight.

The next morning, drain the peas and cover with 1 cup water and 1 cup Sauterne.

Put all of this in a heavy saucepan and bring to a boil. Lower the temperature, cover the pan, and simmer for 30 minutes.

Add salt and ham, and simmer 25 to 30 minutes longer. Add red food coloring. Drain peas, reserving liquid.

Drain and chop the chiles, reserving 2 tbsp. liquid.

Place the peas and ham, chiles, reserved juice from the chiles, tomato juice, onion, and garlic powder in a blender. Blend to make a puree. (If a blender is not available, put mixture through a food mill.) Add a small amount of the liquid reserved from the peas, if needed, to obtain desired consistency.

Spoon the mixture into the top of a double boiler; add the cheese spread and pepper sauce. Cook over medium heat until the cheese melts. Serve warm with crackers or corn chips. *Serves 10-12.*

EGGPLANT APPETIZER À LA JUSTIN

3 small eggplants
Salted water to cover eggplant
    slices
3 tbsp. olive oil
3 tbsp. sifted flour
1 small can tomato sauce
1 rib celery, finely chopped
Small amount of chopped
    parsley
1 cup finely chopped onions
1 small, finely chopped,
    bell pepper

1 clove garlic, finely chopped
1½ cups claret wine or dry
    red wine
1 tbsp. Worcestershire sauce
1 tsp. Louisiana hot sauce
1¼ tsp. salt
1 cup water (if needed)
Additional olive oil
2 cups grated Romano cheese

Peel eggplants, and slice lengthwise in slices from ⅛- to ¼-inch thick. Place slices in salted water, and let them marinate for about 2 hours. (While the eggplant is marinating, the rest of the recipe can be prepared).

Make a roux, with tomato sauce (see my roux recipe). Next, add all the chopped seasonings—celery, parsley, onions, bell pepper, and garlic—to roux, and cook over very low flame for about 20-30 minutes, stirring constantly.

Add wine, Worcestershire sauce, and Louisiana hot sauce to the roux. Salt to taste, approximately 1¼ tsp. Add water if the sauce is too thick. Cook on a slow fire for about 1 hour. When sauce is nearly done, put some olive oil in a frying pan and fry the rinsed and drained eggplant slices to a deep brown.

Arrange slices on a platter, and sprinkle Romano cheese freely. Then spread sauce over the slices. Do this to each layer of eggplant slices. This can be served hot, or you may chill it in refrigerator, then slice it like fudge and serve cold. Many prefer this way of serving. *Serves about 8.*

"If you don' look out, you gonna make this you' entree, because it is so good. Don' you forgot to marinate them eggplant slices in salt water for a couple of hours. If you don' did this, them eggplant might could be bitter."

PARTY CHEESE BALL

2 8-oz. pkg. cream cheese	1 tsp. fresh lemon juice
1 8-oz. pkg. cheddar cheese, grated	2 tsp. Worcestershire sauce
1 tbsp. chopped pimiento	Dash cayenne pepper (or Louisiana hot sauce)
1 tbsp. chopped green pepper	Dash salt
1 tbsp. finely chopped onion	Pecans, finely chopped

Blend together the cream cheese and grated cheddar cheese.
Add all of the other ingredients except the pecans; mix well.
Shape into a ball and roll in the chopped pecans. Wrap, and chill for 24 hours in the refrigerator. Serve with crackers or chips. *Makes one 1½-lb. cheese ball.*

How Many Servings?

You might notice that some of these hors d'oeuvre recipes don't say specifically how many people they will serve. Well, hell, there ain't no way to know how many because some folks just nibble a little bit here and there, while others help themselves like it was the main course!

If you put several different hors d'oeuvres around with lots of crackers and chips, you'll be fine. Just in case, you might make a little extra or have the ingredients on hand to whip up a last-minute extra (that's called *lagniappe* where I come from!). Your family will enjoy the lagniappe the next day, I garontee!

SOUPS AND SALADS

Until I gone and los' me some weights, you ain' gonna got me in that pirogue some at all! (Photo by Bill Cooksey)

TURTLE SOUP À LA MONTELEONE

¾ gal. chicken stock
2 tbsp. cooking oil
1 cup finely chopped green
  onions
⅓ cup finely chopped celery
  (do not use the leaves)
1 cup flour
1 cup tomato sauce

4 hard-boiled eggs, finely
  chopped
¼ cup lemon, finely chopped
Salt and pepper
1 lb. turtle meat, all meat, no
  bones, cut into 1-inch cubes
Sherry wine (when served)

To prepare the stock, boil 2 lb. of chicken in water to cover. When it is done, measure stock, and add water if needed to make ¾ gallon. Refrigerate chicken and any extra stock to use another time. Set cooking pot and stock aside while following next step.

In the oil, sauté onions and celery. Add the flour, and cook and stir until nicely brown. Mix into the stock. Add tomato sauce, hard-boiled eggs, and lemon. Salt and pepper to taste.

Brown the turtle meat, add to the stock, and cook over low flame for 2 hours, covered.

To serve, add sherry wine to individual taste, not more than 1 tbsp. per bowl. *Serves 12.*

"When I go to New Orleans sometime to hear Pete Fountain or maybe Al Hirt, we mos' usual stay at the Hotel Monteleone.

"Sara an' me, we loved that place. I mus' confess that the Monteleone merry-go-roun' bar done make me a little dizzy sometime, but it wort' it, I garontee!

"But maybe what we loved mos' at the Monteleone is they wondermous turtle soup.

"After many years, me an' they chef got ourself acquaint' enough so he tell me how he make this turtle soup.

"An' this recipe is it, only I done add jus' a little something here an' there, which I think make it even better. See if you don' agree with me, huh?"

OYSTER CHOWDER

1 cup diced Irish potatoes
2 tbsp. olive oil
1 cup chopped celery
1 cup chopped onion
½ cup chopped parsley
1 tsp. chopped garlic
3 cups juice from oysters (with water added if necessary)

1 cup Sauterne wine or dry white wine
2 cups oysters
2 tsp. salt
1 tbsp. soy sauce
1 tsp. Louisiana hot sauce

Cook the potatoes until tender.

In the olive oil, sauté celery, onion, and parsley until clear or nearly done. Add garlic. Add the oyster juice and wine to the sautéed vegetables.

Add the potatoes with the water they are in. Bring to a boil, then reduce to a low simmer (about 170 to 175 degrees). Add the oysters, salt, soy sauce, and Louisiana hot sauce.

Let the whole thing simmer for at least 6 hours, or even better, let it simmer overnight. *Serves 6.*

Cajun and Creole Foods

Cajun cooking derived from using the bounty of the land—game, fish, vegetables, and fruit readily available. Frequently, it was one-pot, simple cooking, and it wasn't highly seasoned with hot peppers.

In contrast, Creole cooking was a lot fancier, since it was prepared by the descendants of upper-class French, mainly in New Orleans and surrounding areas. A Creole dinner would have included several courses, would have been elegantly presented, and would have used a greater variety of foods and seasonings than the Cajuns had for their use, although many of the ingredients would have been the same as those used by Cajuns.

SCALLOP CHOWDER

6 tbsp. butter or margarine
1 rib celery, diced
2 onions, diced
2 shallots, diced
1½ lb. peeled, washed, and
   diced potatoes
1 tbsp. salt

Pepper
1 cup Sauterne wine or dry
   white wine
2½ cups water
1 lb. scallops
1 pt. whipping cream
1 tbsp. chopped parsley

In melted butter sauté the celery and onions slowly until the onions are transparent. Add shallots. Blend in potatoes, salt, pepper, wine, and water.

Bring to a boil, and add scallops and their juice, if any. Bring back to a boil, then cut the heat and cook for 10 minutes.

Heat the whipping cream to boiling point in a separate pan. Stir it into the chowder, along with the parsley and a little more salt (if needed). *Serves 10-12.*

That's my wife, Sara, with my good friend, Pat Carroll, the leader of my band. (Photo by David King Gleason)

Seafood Gumbo

2 cups olive oil
5 cups flour
6 cups chopped onion
3 cups chopped bell pepper
2 8-oz. cans tomato sauce
2 cups chopped green onion
½ cup garlic, minced
1½ cups finely chopped
   parsley
6 qt. water
4 tbsp. Worcestershire sauce

3 tbsp. salt (but this may not
   be enough or may be too
   much; taste first, then add.)
2 tsp. cayenne pepper
2 cups Sauterne wine or dry
   white wine
2 doz. crabs
3 lb. shrimp, peeled and
   deveined
Filé powder
Cooked rice

With the olive oil and flour, make a very dark roux (see my roux recipe). Add the onions and bell pepper, stirring constantly until the onions become clear. Pour in the tomato sauce and green onions, and cook until the roux is back to its original dark color. Add garlic, parsley, water, Worcestershire sauce, salt, cayenne pepper, and wine.

Cook the mixture for 45 minutes, then drop in the crabs and shrimp. (Clean the crabs first by placing them in boiling water. Use only the bodies, broken in half, and the large claws.) Let cook for two or more hours.

Filé does not go in the pot! When you're ready to eat, sprinkle the filé over the rice, and cover with steaming hot gumbo. *Serves 15-20.*

Seafood Gumbo with Okra

2 cups okra, cut up
2 large onions, finely chopped
1 medium bell pepper, finely chopped
4 cups Sauterne wine or dry white wine
1 large clove garlic, finely chopped
2 lb. shrimp, shelled

1 pt. crabmeat
1 pt. drained oysters
4 cups water
1 tsp. Louisiana hot sauce
2 tbsp. Worcestershire sauce
4 tsp. salt
Filé powder
Cooked rice

First you make a roux. (Follow my roux recipe.)

Sauté the okra separately. Add onion and bell pepper to the roux, and cook until both are clear or soft.

Add wine, garlic, and the rest of the ingredients. (You should never add garlic to anything until there is some juice or liquid.)

Cook over a low fire for 2 or more hours. When you serve, sprinkle some filé over the rice before putting gumbo over it. *Serves 6-8.*

Filé: Never in the Pot

Filé is a powder made from the leaves of a sassafras tree. You can buy filé in 'mos' any grocery store. It is what makes your gumbo thick enough after it has been cooked. Don't put filé in gumbo until it has cooked. Actually, you should put it in the gumbo when you serve it with the rice.

Filé, what make you' gumbo so good and thick, ain' either a file or a filet. It jus' what it said, filé.

Remember what I done tol' you. Don' put filé in the gumbo while it's cookin'. You don' add the filé to the gumbo in the pot. Jus' sprinkle a little on the gumbo when you dish it up.

An' gumbo is another of them Cajun dishes what tastes even better warmed over the nex' day, if they any lef', which I doubt.

Shrimp and Oyster Gumbo with Filé

Olive oil
1½ cups sifted flour
1 small can tomato sauce
1 small can tomato paste
2 large onions, finely chopped
1 large clove garlic, finely
  chopped
1 medium bell pepper, finely
  chopped
4 cups Sauterne wine or dry
  white wine
Water
2 tsp. Louisiana hot sauce
2 tbsp. Worcestershire sauce
1 to 2 lb. peeled shrimp
1 pint fresh oysters
Salt to taste
Steamed rice

Use large pot that will hold 6 quarts. Make a roux with the olive oil, flour, tomato sauce, and paste (see my roux recipe). Add chopped onions, garlic, and bell pepper. Keep stirring so that mixture will not burn.

Add wine mixed with equal parts of water. This mixture should be thicker than a soup, and additional water should be added to get this consistency. Add Louisiana hot sauce and Worcestershire sauce.

Bring this to a boil, and add shrimp and oysters. Cook on a slow fire for about 2 hours. Salt to taste. Serve with steamed rice. *Serves 8-12.*

If there is any left over, refrigerate or freeze remainder. The leftovers often taste better than when first served.

For crab gumbo, substitute crab bodies and claws. You may also use leftover duck. It makes a wonderful gumbo, too.

More About Filé (pronounced fee-lay)

I used to make my own filé by picking leaves from a sassafras tree in September before they started turning brown. I washed them good and dried them in the sun. You make the filé powder from those leaves. Sassafras trees grow wild throughout South Louisiana. Filé is one of the things the Indians taught the white people how to use.

Filé powder must be used very carefully. If you forget and add it to the gumbo pot, it will make the gumbo stringy. It should be added only as the rice and gumbo are served in individual bowls.

CHICKEN-ANDOUILLE GUMBO À LA ROSINA

1 large stewing chicken
Salt and pepper
1 cup cooking oil
¾ cup all-purpose flour
(for roux)
6 large white or yellow onions,
chopped
1 small bell pepper, chopped
1 tbsp. chopped celery

1 lb. andouille, sliced into
¼-inch slices (gumbo sausage)
6 cups hot water
1 clove garlic, chopped
1 tbsp. finely chopped parsley
1 small bunch green onions,
finely chopped
Salt, black pepper, and
cayenne pepper to taste

Cut up chicken, wash, and season with salt and pepper.

Heat 1 cup oil in heavy skillet, and fry chicken until brown. Remove chicken and put aside.

Pour remaining oil from the skillet into large heavy pot and, using the flour, make a roux without tomatoes (see my recipe).

After roux is made, lower heat, and add the white onions, bell pepper, and celery. Cover and simmer until onions are clear, stirring occasionally.

Add sliced andouille and chicken to roux mixture, cover and let simmer about ½ hour. Stir often during this process. Keep heat low through this point.

Add water, garlic, parsley and green onions. You may increase heat until mixture begins to boil. Now lower heat to simmer, cover, and cook 1½ to 2 hours or until chicken is tender. Before serving, season with salt, black pepper, and cayenne pepper. *Serves 10-12.*

This has a lot of liquid and is served in a bowl over rice, over which ¼ tsp. filé has been sprinkled. It's even better the next day.

This recipe may also be used for duck, rabbit, and squirrel. In making seafood gumbo, such as with shrimp, crab, or oysters, the only difference, of course, is that there will be no frying of the particular seafood being used.

Who dat say I don' got me a pot to cook in? — An' me, I got the window, too! (Photo by Bill Cooksey)

CHICKEN GUMBO

1 large onion, finely chopped
1 large clove garlic, finely
   chopped
4 cups Sauterne wine or dry
   white wine
4 cups water
2 tbsp. Worcestershire sauce

1 2-lb. chicken, cut up
1 fresh hot pepper or 1 tsp.
   Louisiana hot sauce
1 lb. andouille sausage,
   cut into ¼-inch slices
Salt to taste

First you make a roux (see my roux recipe).

Add all of the ingredients to the roux, and simmer until the chicken and sausage are done. It's some good, I garontee! *Serves 10-12.*

"The trouble wit' people is dey don' know what andouille sausage is. It's sausage used for makin' gumbo, like dis chicken gumbo. Or use it wit' rice or Irish potatoes. It's damn good eatin' sausage wit' anyt'ing. A pine burr taste good wit' andouille. Dare ain't no question about dat, no!"

OKRA GUMBO

When making okra gumbo, you may use chicken or any of the variations mentioned for Chicken-Andouille Gumbo à la Rosina. Follow the same directions, using the same ingredients, but add:

2 cups chopped okra

2 large, peeled fresh tomatoes or 1 16-oz. can tomatoes

To add these two ingredients, grease a heavy skillet (preferably aluminum), sauté chopped okra, stirring often, for about 20 minutes, then add tomatoes and, while stirring, mash the tomatoes so that they mix well with okra. It is not necessary to use tomatoes. You may use only okra, if you prefer.

You may add these ingredients, as in Chicken-Andouille Gumbo, just before adding the water:

1 clove garlic, chopped
1 tbsp. finely chopped parsley

1 small bunch green onions, finely chopped

Seafood Soup

1 cup celery, chopped
1 onion, chopped
1 green onion, chopped
1 cup bell pepper, chopped
1 lime, chopped
1 clove garlic, finely chopped
1 cup cubed carrots
2 tbsp. dried parsley (or 1 cup fresh)

3 cups raw fish, boned and cubed
2 cups crawfish, shrimp, crabmeat, or oysters
½ tsp. cayenne pepper
Salt to taste

Combine all of the vegetables, and cover with about 1 inch of water. Boil until tender.

Add the fish and crawfish; boil with the seasonings until cooked well. (Shrimp, crabmeat, or oysters may be used instead of crawfish.)

I think it's a good idea to boil the soup for approximately 30 minutes, then simmer for 1½ hours. *Serves 6-8.*

"Then you will got you some fine tastin' soup, I garontee!"

Avocado Soup

2 cups chopped avocado
1 tsp. salt
1½ cups chicken stock (or canned chicken broth)

1 tbsp. Worcestershire sauce
Dash Louisiana hot sauce
2 cups buttermilk

Put all of the ingredients in a blender and liquefy. Refrigerate. Serve cold. *Serves 6.*

Red Bean Soup

See recipe for Dried Red Beans, or use any that are left over. After beans are cooked, mash well or put through a colander. Add water to consistency of thick soup. Serve with croutons.

VEGETABLE SOUP

Get a good piece of soup meat, preferably a beef brisket with fat, because that's where the flavor is.

Cover meat with water. See what you have in your pantry or your refrigerator to put in there, such as:

Sliced carrots   **English peas**
Turnips   **Whole-grain corn**
Potatoes   **Celery**
Butter beans

Use any kind of vegetable you have! Add parsley, salt, and Louisiana hot sauce to taste. Bring to a boil.

Let it simmer for about 2 hours. Sprinkle filé on top when you serve. (Filé is green sassafras leaves that are ground and dried. And will it add flavor! Ooh boy!)

CHILI I

4 lb. chili meat, ground coarsely   **2 cups chopped onion**
   or cut into small pieces   **1 cup chopped bell pepper**
Bacon drippings (or olive oil)   **1 clove garlic, chopped**
1 6-pack beer   **Louisiana hot sauce**
2 tbsp. chili powder   **Salt to taste**
2 tbsp. Hershey's cocoa

Brown the meat in bacon drippings or olive oil.

Add the beer, chili powder, cocoa, and other ingredients. Let cook at least an hour. An' it's better if you let it cook slowly for 3 hours. *Serves 6-8.*

"It's delicious! And you can't taste the cocoa!"

CHILI II

4 lb. chili meat, ground coarsely or cut into small pieces	2 tbsp. Hershey's cocoa
Bacon drippings (or olive oil)	2 cups chopped onion
4 cups Sauterne wine or dry white wine	1 cup chopped bell pepper
4 cups water	1 clove garlic, chopped
2 tbsp. chili powder	Louisiana hot sauce
	Salt to taste

Brown the meat in bacon drippings or olive oil.

Add the wine and water.

Add the rest of the ingredients, and let cook for at least an hour. Again, it's better if you cook it for 3 hours. *Serves 6-8.*

SALAD À LA WILSON

2 avocados	2 tsp. Worcestershire sauce
2 heaping tbsp. salad dressing	1 tsp. Louisiana hot sauce
4 tbsp. olive oil	1 tsp. salt
3 tbsp. wine vinegar	

Peel and cut avocados in half.

Mix the other ingredients well, and pour over the avocados. *Serves 6.*

Dis lady here is Mrs. Audrey Scivique. She got a fine restaurant down where I used to live, and dat ain't all. She's a damn good cook, too, you hear? (Photo by David King Gleason)

HAM SALAD STUFFED TOMATOES

1½ cups finely diced baked ham
½ cup finely diced celery
¼ cup chopped pecans
2 tbsp. chopped pimiento-
 stuffed olives
1 tbsp. finely chopped, peeled
 onion

¼ cup mayonnaise
1 tbsp. chili sauce
4 medium-sized tomatoes
Crisp lettuce leaves
Fresh parsley sprigs

Mix together the ham, celery, pecans, olives, and onion in a large bowl. Stir in the mayonnaise and chili sauce.

Placing the stem end down on a board, cut each tomato about two-thirds of the way down into 8 wedges. Gently push wedges open to allow space for stuffing.

Place each tomato on a lettuce-lined salad plate, and stuff with equal amounts of the ham salad. Garnish plates with parsley. *Serves 4.*

RED BEAN SALAD

2 cans red beans
1 medium onion, chopped
1 cup celery, chopped
½ cup dill pickles, chopped
2 hard-boiled eggs, finely
 chopped

2 heaping tbsp. mayonnaise
Salt and pepper to taste
1 tbsp. Worcestershire sauce
 (optional)
Louisiana hot sauce (optional)

Cook red beans or use canned ones—I prefer canned ones for this as they stay whole better. Drain well.

Add chopped onions, celery, pickles, and finely chopped eggs. Toss with mayonnaise. Salt and pepper to taste. I like Worcestershire sauce and Louisiana hot sauce in this. Great with barbecue of any kind. *Serves 6-8.*

LOBSTER SALAD

4 cups cooked lobster
  (or crawfish)
3 hard-boiled eggs, chopped
½ cup celery
¼ cup chopped green onions

2 crisp apples, peeled, cored,
  and diced
1 banana, sliced
Mayonnaise
¼ cup sour cream

Toss together lightly (so as not to mash) everything except the mayonnaise and sour cream.

Add the mayonnaise, lightened with ¼ cup sour cream. Serve with banana bread or plantain chips. *Serves 6-8.*

RICE SALAD

2 cups rice
1 cup green onions, chopped
1 cup dill pickle, chopped
1 cup sweet pickle, chopped
1 cup celery, chopped
1 cup bell pepper, chopped
1 cup olives (with pimiento),
  chopped
1½ cups finely chopped hard-
  boiled eggs

1 cup salad dressing
3 to 4 tbsp. Durkee's Famous
  Sauce
3 tbsp. prepared yellow
  mustard
Cayenne pepper to taste
Olive oil
3 dashes wine vinegar

Cook the rice according to the directions on the package.

Combine in a bowl the onion, pickles, celery, bell pepper, olives, egg, and cooked rice.

Mix together thoroughly the salad dressing, Durkee's, mustard, cayenne pepper, olive oil, and wine vinegar. Blend in with the dry ingredients.

Refrigerate the whole darn mess. *Serves 8.*

"By the way, this is better if refrigerated and served the next day."

Marinated Green Beans

French Salad Dressing à la Justin
1 small wedge of bleu cheese, mashed
2 cans vertical-packed green beans

1 small can pimiento, cut into strips
2 medium onions, sliced

Make French dressing (see recipe below).

Add the bleu cheese that has been mashed, and mix well.

Put green beans, pimiento, and onions in a bowl, and toss with this dressing. Cover, and place in refrigerator overnight. *Serves 6.*

Some people may not care for bleu cheese, and this can be eliminated. If any beans are left over, these can be added to a tossed green salad and are very good.

French Salad Dressing à la Justin

1 medium clove garlic, whole
Salt
½ cup olive oil
2 tsp. Worcestershire sauce

½ tsp. Louisiana hot sauce
½ lemon
¼ cup wine vinegar

Cover garlic amply with salt, and mash with fork to fine pulp, taking up all of the salt. Add olive oil, stir well.

Add Worcestershire sauce and hot sauce, and stir well. Squeeze juice from ½ lemon around sides so that it runs down into sauce. Stir well.

Add wine vinegar, and stir briskly. *Serves 6.*

Use on any green salad or tomato and lettuce.

Molded Green Beans Amandine

2 8-oz. pkg. softened cream
    cheese
2 10½-oz. cans condensed
    chicken broth
3 10-oz. pkg. frozen cut green
    beans, cooked until tender

1 cup finely chopped parsley
2 tbsp. lemon juice
2 envelopes plain gelatin
1 cup water
¾ cup toasted slivered almonds
Parsley

Beat cheese until soft; mix in the undiluted chicken broth.

Fold in the cooked green beans, parsley, and lemon juice.

Soften the gelatin in water in a small saucepan, then stir over low heat until dissolved. Stir into the salad mixture.

Toast almonds in a shallow pan at 400 degrees for 5 minutes. Add hot almonds to the salad.

Turn the mixture into a 2½-quart mold, and chill until set.

Unmold onto plate, and garnish with parsley. *Serves 6-8.*

Hot Slaw

2 strips bacon, cut into small
    pieces
1 large onion, chopped
1 bell pepper, chopped

1 small cabbage, shredded
2 cans whole tomatoes
Salt and black pepper
Cayenne pepper

Fry bacon until crisp, then sauté onions and bell pepper until clear.

Add cabbage, and mix well.

Add tomatoes, salt, black, and cayenne pepper to taste. Let simmer 45 minutes. (Some like to add 1 tablespoon vinegar for tartness.) *Serves 6-8.*

COLD SLAW

5 heaping tbsp. mayonnaise
2 heaping tbsp. Durkee's
   Famous Sauce
2 tbsp. olive oil
1 tsp. Louisiana hot sauce
2 tbsp. catsup
Salt
½ to 1 tsp. garlic salt

1 tbsp. wine vinegar
Juice from 1 lemon
1 large, hard head of cabbage,
   shredded
2 medium onions, sliced into
   thin onion rings
Salt and pepper to taste

Put mayonnaise and Durkee's in a bowl large enough to hold complete mixture, but shaped so that it can be beaten with a fork. Beat mayonnaise and Durkee's until combined, add olive oil slowly, beating all the while. Beat until mixture has returned to thickness of original mayonnaise.

Add Louisiana hot sauce, continuing to beat. Add catsup, keep beating. Add salt and garlic salt, beating all the time. Add wine vinegar; this will thin the sauce down. Beat this thoroughly, adding the lemon juice as you do so.

Taste for salt and pepper, keeping in mind that you have to salt and pepper the slaw with this mixture. Therefore, it can be a little saltier than if you were just eating the sauce alone.

Place shredded cabbage and onion rings in large salad bowl. Pour sauce over, and toss well. This should be done about an hour before serving. *Serves 8-10.*

If you don' taste while you' cookin', how you gonna know it good?
Anyway, me, I got my hungers up all the time. (Photo by Bill Cooksey)

MEATS

What did you said? Cook without wine? C'mon now, how you gonna did that, huh? (Photo by Bill Cooksey)

BAKED CUBED STEAK

Olive oil
1 4- or 5-lb. heavy beef steak,
   1½ to 2 inches thick, cut into
   3-inch squares
3-4 tbsp. flour
1 medium onion, finely
   chopped
1 clove garlic, finely chopped

1½ cups water
2 tbsp. Justin Wilson Steak
   Sauce
Louisiana hot sauce to taste
1½ cups claret wine or dry red
   wine
Salt to taste

Among the meats that may be used for this recipe are sirloin, round, T-bone, chuck, loin tip. If round steak is used, it will have to cook a little longer than the choicer cuts.

Cover bottom of skillet with olive oil, and sear steak squares on all sides.

Remove from skillet, and place in baking pan. Add flour to the fat left in the skillet, turning the fire down so that it will cook slowly. Stir the flour constantly, and if the mixture of fat and flour is too dry, add some more olive oil.

Preheat the oven to 400 degrees.

Cook and stir until mixture is a rich brown. Add onions and garlic, stirring all the while, and then pour in the water. Stir this until it starts to form a thick gravy. Add steak sauce and Louisiana hot sauce to taste. Add more water if necessary to prevent burning when you are bringing it to a boil.

Add wine and salt to taste, and pour mixture over steak squares.

Bake in the preheated oven for 30-45 minutes, basting frequently. Add water if needed. *Serves 4-6.*

SHOULDER BEEF STEAK ETOUFFÉE

3 ½- to ¾-inch-thick shoulder
  steaks
Lemon-pepper seasoning
Salt
Cayenne pepper
2 tsp. garlic, finely chopped
3 slices lime, chopped

2 cups chopped onion
1 cup chopped bell pepper
Soy sauce
1 cup Sauterne wine or dry
  white wine
Parsley

Season meat with lemon pepper, salt, cayenne pepper, and garlic. Put the meat in a pot, and add the rest of the ingredients.

Cover and cook over a low fire. Get it real hot to start, then turn down and cook it slowly until the meat is done. And it is delicious! *Serves 6-8.*

Etouffée (eh-too-fey)

Over the years, I've learned about many kinds of étouffée. The word means "smothered," or cooked down in a thick sauce.

I once made an étouffée of nine hundred pounds of turtle meat for a man in Texas who had a construction company. I used several iron pots, which are the best pots to cook in because they bring out all the good flavors.

You don't put a lot of liquid in étouffée. Just put a lid on it, and let it cook down. People think you've got to make a roux, but you don't make a roux for étouffée. You can étouffée anything—crawfish, turtle, seven steaks, rabbit, squirrel. They are all delicious, I garontee!

SEVEN STEAKS ETOUFFÉE

2 tbsp. cooking oil
7 steaks (or 1 round steak, making 4 pounds total)
2 6-oz. cans mushroom steak sauce
1 cup Sauterne wine or dry white wine
1 cup chopped onion
¼ cup chopped pimiento

2 tsp. chopped garlic
1 tsp. celery seed
1 tbsp. dried parsley
1 tbsp. soy sauce
¼ tbsp. bitters (Peychaud or Angostura)
1 tsp. Louisiana hot sauce
Salt and pepper to taste

Heat the cooking oil in a Dutch oven. Add the meat, and cover with the rest of the ingredients. Salt and pepper to taste.

Cover and let cook over low heat for 2-3 hours. *Serves 6-8.*

CORNED BEEF AND CABBAGE AU VIN

3-5 lb. corned beef
Water
4 cups Sauterne wine or dry white wine
2 tbsp. Worcestershire sauce

1 cayenne pepper or dash Louisiana hot sauce
1 large cabbage
4 large onions (whole)
Salt to taste

Cover corned beef with water. Add wine, Worcestershire sauce, and cayenne pepper. Boil until tender (about 2 or 3 hours).

Remove corned beef.

Cut cabbage into quarters, and add to stock with whole onions. Boil until tender. Salt to taste. *Serves 6-8.*

STUFFED PEPPERS, CAJUN STYLE

8 green bell peppers
1 cup yellow cornmeal
½ cup Sauterne wine or dry
  white wine
½ cup water
1½ lb. lean ground beef
1 clove garlic, mashed
1 tbsp. chili powder
1 1-lb. can kidney beans, well
  drained

1 egg, well beaten
1½ tsp. salt
1 tsp. cayenne pepper
1 cup minced onion
½ cup tomato sauce
¼ cup chopped pimiento
½ cup dry bread crumbs
8 strips bacon

Preheat the oven to 325 degrees.

Slice the tops from the peppers, and remove seeds.

Cook cornmeal into a mush in the wine and water. (Add more water if necessary.)

Spoon the mush into the peppers, spreading mush to line each.

Combine the remaining ingredients, except bacon, blend well, and stuff into the peppers.

Place peppers side by side in a shallow pan, and top with bacon strips. Add about 1 inch of water to the pan.

Bake, uncovered, in the preheated oven for 1 hour, or until done. Serve hot. *Serves 8.*

SWEETBREADS VEAU AUX CHAMPIGNONS À LA PIERRE

4 lb. sweetbreads
3 tbsp. olive oil
½ cup flour
2½ medium onions, chopped
2 cloves garlic, chopped

2 cups water
2½ cups Beaujolais (or any dry
  red wine)
1 medium can mushrooms

Clean sweetbreads, making sure to remove any excess skin. Cut into chunks.

Put the olive oil in large pot (preferably iron), and place sweetbreads in cold oil. Brown sweetbreads over medium fire and remove them from the pot.

Add flour to olive oil remaining in pot (if necessary, add a little more oil), and turn fire down low. Stir constantly until ingredients are thoroughly mixed.

When the roux becomes dark, almost burnt-looking, add chopped onions and chopped garlic. When these are browned, add water and wine.

Return sweetbreads to the simmering pot. Turn fire up to medium heat, and cook for ½ hour, then add mushrooms. Cook for another ½ hour. Good with steamed rice. *Serves 6-8.*

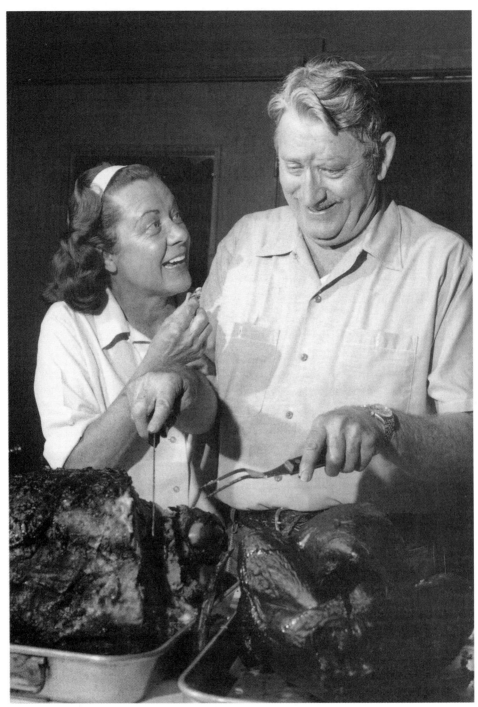

My wife, Sara, liked the taste of this roast, as you can tell by the look on her face. (Photo by David King Gleason)

ROAST BEEF

1 10-lb. heavy beef rump roast
  (with big bone removed)
6 small green onions
6 cloves garlic
6 green hot peppers
Salt

Cayenne pepper
3 tbsp. olive oil
3 cups claret wine or dry red
  wine
Water
1 cup coarsely chopped onions

Preheat the oven to 400 degrees.

Punch holes in roast, and stuff a 1-inch piece of onion, a garlic clove, and a pepper in each hole, along with a little salt. Rub salt and cayenne pepper all over the roast.

Heat olive oil in roaster on top of stove. When hot enough, sear all sides of roast in the olive oil.

Pour the wine and a little water in roaster, and add chopped onions.

Place covered roaster in the preheated oven and baste occasionally. Cook 2½ hours for roast with medium-rare center—longer if well-done meat is desired. *Serves 8-10.*

I wanna tol' you, dat devilish gleam what I got in ma eye is to let you know dat ain't catsup I'm pourin' on dat meat, no. Dat's ground red cayenne pepper, an' ooh, whee! It's got some seasoning on dat. Not too hot, jus' rat. (Photo by David King Gleason)

BARBECUED ROAST OF BEEF

10- to 15-lb. heavy beef round roast
6-8 cloves garlic
6-8 green onions
6-8 green hot peppers (cayenne)

Salt
Ground cayenne pepper
Olive oil
2 cups Sauterne wine

Start fire in covered barbecue pit, using charcoal, not briquettes. Have fire going for about 30 minutes before meat is placed on it, then keep a slow fire going by adding charcoal when needed and also an occasional stick of wet hickory or pecan wood.

Puncture holes in the roast so you can put a clove of garlic, a green onion, and a hot pepper in each hole. Rub salt and ground cayenne pepper into the meat on all sides.

Put enough olive oil in the bottom of a large baking pan to cover bottom well. Place roast in pan, and put pan on barbecue fire.

Close lid on the pit, and let roast sear, turning to get all sides. (With a round roast, it is difficult to sear more than two sides.)

As soon as the roast is seared, pour wine into pan, not on the roast. Baste meat frequently with its own juices, and turn it often.

Cook for about 6-8 hours on a slow fire. If fire blazes up, sprinkle a little water on it. However, if fire is properly kept and pit is kept closed most of the time, blazing should not be a problem. If any additional juice is needed, mix ½ wine and ½ water and add to pan. *Serves 10-12.*

SHORT-RIB SPAGHETTI DINNER

7 beef short ribs (about 5
   pounds untrimmed)
2 medium onions, sliced
2 tsp. salt
½ tsp. pepper
1 tsp. sugar
1 tsp. whole allspice
4 small bay leaves
2 beef bouillon cubes
2 cups hot water

1 8-oz. pkg. spaghetti
2 10-oz. pkg. frozen peas
1 15½-oz. can onions
2 tbsp. melted butter or margarine
Paprika
Grated Parmesan cheese
2 tbsp. flour
1 tsp. sugar

About 2½ hours before serving time, heat large greased Dutch oven until very hot. Add ribs, fat side down, and cook over medium heat until well browned, about 30 minutes.

Lay sliced onions in fat around meat, and cook a minute or so, or until browned.

Add salt, pepper, 1 tsp. sugar, allspice, bay leaves, bouillon cubes, and 2 cups hot water. Simmer, covered, from 1½ to 2 hours until ribs are tender.

Cook spaghetti.

Cook peas.

Heat large serving platter. Warm canned onions and toss in the melted butter.

Drain spaghetti, heap in center of platter, put short ribs around edge, alternating spoonfuls of peas, onions, and ribs. Sprinkle peas and onions with paprika. Sprinkle Parmesan cheese on spaghetti, if desired.

Skim fat from liquid. Slowly stir in ½ cup cold water, blended with flour and 1 tsp. sugar. Cook until thickened and pass as gravy. *Serves 8.*

Barbecued Pork or Beef Ribs

RIBS

Pork ribs and/or beef ribs	**Cayenne pepper**
Salt	

Salt and pepper ribs and place on barbecue pit. Keep fire low.

BASTING SAUCE

Beer	**Cooked Barbecue Sauce**
Water	
1 tsp. or 2 dashes	
Worcestershire sauce to	
each bottle of beer	

Make basting sauce by mixing beer with an equal amount of water and 1 tsp. or 2 dashes of Worcestershire sauce to each bottle of beer. Make basting sauce as needed. Baste ribs and turn frequently, basting before and after turning.

Just before ribs are ready to come off, baste both sides twice with my Cooked Barbecue Sauce (see my recipe). Remember, pork must be well done.

If you prefer crisp, dry barbecued ribs, just use basting sauce; eliminate final barbecue sauce.

"On a rainy day, this same effect can nearly be reached in your own oven by adding 2 or 3 drops of Liquid Smoke to the basting sauce."

PORK CHOPS WITH DRESSING

2 cups bread crumbs
2 eggs
1 cup claret wine or dry
   red wine
¼ cup olive oil
1 large onion, juiced or grated
2 cloves garlic, juiced or
   pressed
½ small bay leaf, broken into
   tiny pieces

2 tbsp. Justin Wilson Steak
   Sauce
1½ tsp. Louisiana cayenne hot
   sauce
Salt and ground cayenne
   pepper
6 pork chops, ¾-inch thick

Preheat the oven to 350 degrees.

Put bread crumbs in a mixing bowl. Into this beat eggs, and add a cup of wine, then the olive oil. Add onion, garlic, and bay leaf. Mix well.

Then add steak sauce and Louisiana hot sauce, and mix well again. This mixture should be juicy and not dry. Add wine if it seems too dry, and add bread crumbs if too wet. Salt to taste.

Use a casserole dish large enough to lay pork chops in a single layer and deep enough to hold the above mixture. Grease the casserole with olive oil, and pour the dressing in it. Smooth it out, and lay salted, cayenne-peppered pork chops on top. Bake in the preheated oven until done. *Serves 6.*

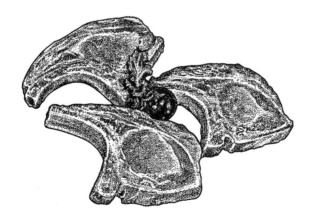

BROILED PORK CHOPS AU VIN

10 pork chops, ¾-inch thick
Salt
Cayenne pepper
¼ cup olive oil
2 green onions
2 cloves garlic

2 cups Sauterne or claret wine
1 cup water
1 tbsp. Worcestershire sauce
1 tsp. Louisiana hot sauce
½ tsp. salt
Juice from ½ lemon

Salt and pepper both sides of pork chops.

Cover bottom of baking pan with olive oil—a generous covering—and also rub oil on sides of pan.

Place pork chops in baking pan, and cook in broiler until done. Length of broiling time depends on thickness of meat.

While chops are broiling, dice green onions and garlic very fine. Heat a little oil in a skillet and sauté until soft, not done. Add wine and water to sautéed onions and garlic. Add Worcestershire, hot sauce, ½ tsp. salt, and the juice of ½ lemon. Simmer.

While onions are being sautéed, pork chops should be turned. When both sides are brown, take pork chops from broiler, and pour the sautéed onion mixture over them.

Bake at 350 to 400 degrees for about 30 to 40 minutes, or until the gravy is done. Serve the gravy over steamed rice or creamed potatoes. *Serves 4-5.*

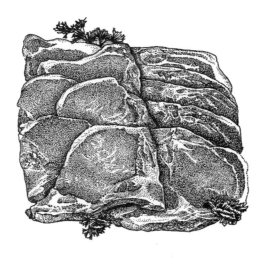

CAJUNIZED ORIENTAL PORK CHOPS

6 thick pork chops
Salt and cayenne pepper
1½ cups Sauterne wine or dry
  white wine
1 cup chopped bell pepper

1 cup chopped onion
1 clove garlic, chopped
3 tbsp. soy sauce
1 15-oz. can pineapple chunks

Salt and pepper the chops, and brown them slowly in a skillet.
Add wine, bell pepper, onion, and garlic.
Cover and simmer for 25 to 30 minutes.
Remove pork chops, being sure to keep them warm.
Add the soy sauce and syrup from the pineapple. Stir until more or less thick. Add the pineapple chunks, and bring to a boil. Serve over pork chops and hot cooked rice. *Serves 6.*

BAKED PORK CHOPS WITH RICE AND TOMATOES

6 1-inch-thick pork chops
Salt
Pepper
1 large bell pepper
2 cups cooked rice

1 medium onion, sliced
1 large tomato (fresh or
  canned)
2 no. 3 (about 4 cups ea.) cans
  tomatoes

In large skillet, brown the pork chops that have been seasoned with salt and pepper. Arrange meat in large baking dish so each pork chop will be on the bottom.
Preheat the oven to 375 degrees.
Clean bell pepper and slice into rings, then place one on each pork chop. With ice-cream scoop or large spoon, dip rice, pat until firm, and place in bell-pepper ring. Place slice of onion on each, and top with tomato slice.
Chop canned tomatoes up fine. Season with salt and pepper, and pour around pork chops.
Cover and steam 1 hour in the preheated oven. This is pretty as well as good. *Serves 6.*

Baked and Broiled Pork Chops

6 pork chops
Salt
Ground cayenne pepper

1 cup Sauterne wine or dry
  white wine
1 tbsp. soy sauce

Preheat oven to 350 degrees. Grease pan.

Salt and pepper the pork chops on both sides. Put in the preheated oven for 10 minutes.

Mix wine and soy sauce together and pour over the pork chops when they begin to brown.

Set oven on broil. Broil the pork chops until browned on both sides. *Serves 6.*

Super-Sized Kraut-Stuffed Chops

2 tbsp. olive oil
6 thick loin pork chops with
  pockets
2 green peppers
1 cup chopped onion
1 lb. carrots, peeled and
  shredded

1½ tsp. salt
¼ tsp. pepper
¼ tsp. dried mint
1 tbsp. sugar
6 cups drained sauerkraut

Brown the chops on both sides in olive oil in a large ovenproof skillet. Remove chops and set aside.

Slice 4 rings from the green peppers and set aside; dice remaining green pepper.

Preheat the oven to 325 degrees.

Sauté the diced pepper and onion in drippings until clear. Stir in carrots, and sauté 1 minute. Add seasonings, sugar, and sauerkraut; toss until combined.

Stuff each pork chop with some of the kraut mixture. Use small skewers or sew with heavy thread to close the opening.

Place stuffed pork chops on top of the remaining kraut mixture in a baking pan. Cover and bake in the preheated oven for 45 minutes; uncover and bake 40 minutes longer or until chops are done.

Remove skewers or thread from chops before serving. Garnish with green pepper rings. *Serves 6.*

OVEN PORK ROAST

1 8- to 10-lb. center-cut   Water
   pork-loin roast   Chopped green-onion tops
Salt and pepper

Preheat the oven to 400 degrees.

Salt and pepper roast well, and place on rack in roasting pan with 1 inch water in bottom of pan. Cover and cook in the oven until almost done (about 2½ hours). Baste occasionally, and add more water if needed.

Uncover roaster, score fatty side of roast, pat green-onion tops all over the top, and cook uncovered until browned. *Serves 12.*

GOOD OL' SAUSAGE

5 lb. lean pork meat   ⅛ lb. fine salt
2½ lb. clear fat pork   ½ tsp. pepper
½ tsp. sugar   ¼ tsp. dried mint
¼ tsp. ginger

Cut meat into small pieces, and season with sugar, ginger, salt, pepper, and mint. Put through a food chopper, using the sausage cutter, and grind twice.

Pack into sterilized jars, and keep in a cool place. Use as wanted. This can be frozen, too. *Serves 6-8.*

ROAST PORK WITH APPLEKRAUT

1 rolled pork-loin roast, 2½ to 3
  pounds
½ tsp. garlic powder
1 tsp. salt
1 tsp. cayenne pepper
1 tsp. dried mint
½ cup butter or margarine

4 medium cooking apples,
  cored and sliced into rings
4 cups drained sauerkraut
  (2 16-oz. cans)
½ cup packed light brown
  sugar

Preheat the oven to 325 degrees.

Sprinkle meat with garlic powder, salt, pepper, and mint.

Place the meat on a rack in an open roasting pan. Roast in the pre-heated oven for 2 hours. Remove the roast from oven, and let it stand 15 minutes for easier carving; remove strings.

Meanwhile, melt the butter in a large skillet. Add the apple rings, a few at a time, and cook until well browned. Stir in the remaining ingredients. Cover and cook over low heat 30 minutes, stirring occasionally.

Serve kraut mixture with sliced roast pork. *Serves 6.*

"Dis jus' got to be good. Dat's all dare is to it. If some of you friens' don't like dat I t'ink dey better call the doctor quick an' fast 'cause dey is plumb sick."

Backbone and Turnips

½ cup bacon drippings
3 to 4 lb. pork backbone
3 cups onion
1 cup bell pepper
1 cup celery
½ cup parsley
1 tsp. garlic

2 tsp. Worcestershire sauce
Ground cayenne pepper
8 cups chopped turnips
3 tsp. salt
1 cup Sauterne wine or dry
   white wine
Water

First you make a roux. (See my roux recipe.)

Brown the backbone off in bacon drippings in a Dutch oven.

Add onion, bell pepper, celery, and parsley to the roux. After you get some juice, add the garlic. Add the remaining ingredients, including the browned backbone, and pour enough water over it to cover.

Cook 3-4 hours over medium heat. *Serves 6-8.*

Barbecued Ham

8- to 10-lb. precooked ham
6 green onions
3 cloves garlic

3 hot peppers (cayenne, chile
   cortillas, etc.)
Cooked Barbecue sauce

Preheat the oven to 400 degrees.

With a sharp knife, score ham and punch holes in it, spacing the holes so you will have about 6.

In each hole, stuff one piece green onion, ½ clove garlic, ½ hot pepper.

Place ham in baking pan. Do not cover. Pour Cooked Barbecue Sauce (see recipe) over ham liberally, leaving at least 1 inch of barbecue sauce in bottom of pan.

Place in the preheated oven or in covered barbecue pit over slow fire, and cook for about 1½ hours. Use charcoal, not briquettes, and add some hickory chips if barbecue pit is used. *Serves 12.*

GLAZED HAM LOAF

1½ lb. fresh ground pork
1 lb. ground smoked ham
1 cup fine dry bread crumbs
1 tsp. salt
¾ tsp. prepared mustard
1 cup milk
2 eggs, well beaten
2 tbsp. finely chopped green
  pepper

½ cup brown sugar
½ cup water
¼ cup white vinegar
1 tbsp. dry mustard
½ cup Sauterne wine or dry
  white wine

Preheat the oven to 325 degrees.

Blend pork, ham, bread crumbs, salt, prepared mustard, milk, eggs, and green pepper. More green pepper may be added if desired.

Shape mixture into a loaf; score the top in a diagonal crisscross pattern. Place in a well-greased, large, shallow baking dish.

Combine the remaining ingredients in a small saucepan. Bring to a boil, stirring often. Pour the sauce over the loaf.

Bake in the preheated oven for 2 hours, basting occasionally. Serve the sauce over the loaf. *Serves 8.*

Cajun Communities

People tend to assume that all Cajuns live around Lafayette and Southwest Louisiana, but you'll find Cajun communities all along the Mississippi River, too.

They didn't all arrive in Louisiana at the same time, and many of them settled in Donaldsonville, White Castle, Lutcher, and on up to Independence, Amite, and Hammond.

There were a lot of Germans in some of these communities, and if it hadn't've been for them, the Cajuns would have starved to death. The Germans taught them a lot about survival, as did the Indians. We lived near Amite, and Mama was a Cajun lady, which makes me a half-Cajun gentleman!

I wonder who oversmoked this turkey! (Photo by David King Gleason)

TURKEY AND HAM IN THE SMOKER COOKER

1 turkey	Shallots
1 apple	½ tsp. bitters (Peychaud or
2 onions	Angostura)
Whole garlic cloves	1 tbsp. Liquid Smoke
Salt	2 tbsp. Worcestershire sauce
Ground cayenne pepper	2 cups Sauterne wine or dry
1 ham	white wine
Hot green peppers	Water

Cut the apple and one onion in half, and stuff them in the turkey. Put a few whole garlic cloves in the turkey. Salt and pepper to taste.

Cut holes in the ham, and stuff each with garlic, green peppers, and shallots. Do this in various places on both sides.

Meanwhile, build the fire for the smoker cooker, and get the charcoal going. Put hickory chips on the top.

Place in the pan the other onion, 2 cloves garlic, the bitters, Liquid Smoke, Worcestershire sauce, and wine. Add water.

Put your turkey in the cooker first, and then the ham on top, so the fat from the ham will drip down and flavor the turkey.

Cook for 18 hours. Also, be sure you have water in the cooker at all times. It you don't, it will just dry out completely. Check the fire, too, because it may not last that long. *Serves about 20.*

"Put the pan in there before you rekindle the fire, or the fire will go out. I've done it many a time, and it makes me so mad I couldn't spit."

ROAST LEG OF LAMB

1 leg of lamb
5 cloves garlic
6 green onions
6 pickled or fresh hot peppers
Salt
Cayenne pepper

3 tbsp. dried mint
Olive oil
1 tbsp. Worcestershire sauce
4 cups Sauterne wine or dry
    white wine

Preheat the oven to 400 degrees.

Wipe leg of lamb well with dry cloth.

Using sharp knife, punch 6 holes in leg of lamb. In each hole, place garlic clove, green onion, and either pickled or fresh hot pepper.

Salt leg of lamb well, and pepper it with cayenne pepper. Pat the dried mint flakes on entire leg of lamb.

Put enough olive oil in a baking pan to keep lamb from burning. Place the lamb in baking pan, put in the preheated oven, and sear the lamb on all sides.

After the lamb is seared, add the Worcestershire sauce and 4 cups Sauterne wine. Baste lamb frequently, and if any additional juice is needed, add half wine and half water.

Continue baking at 400 degrees to your taste, approximately 2 hours. *Serves 8-10.*

Tips on Buying and Cooking Lamb

"You axe almos' any ex-GI what was in Australia during Worl' War Twice an' he gonna told you that of all his unfavorite meats, lamb or mutton is his unfavorist.

"To tell the trut', I don't t'ink dat Australian mutton was mutton a'tall. It was some kind of ol' mountain goat. Hooey! Did that stuff ever have an aroma, one you ain't never gonna forgot!

"But this leg of lamb is different, I garontee! In the firs' place, it is young, tender lamb, not tough ol' mutton. And, most important, is the way we cook this lamb.

"The wine and the mint is what make the difference. If you have any trouble gettin' that mint to stay on the lamb, jus' mix it up wit' the wine and Worcestershire sauce, and it gonna stick, good.

"When you buy leg of lamb, be sure and get you' butcher to remove the leg glands for you. An' when you serve this dish, even to an ex-GI, you gonna hear them raves."

Peggy Bercegeay and me, making each other laugh. He loved the song "Peggy O'Neil" and always played it on the jukebox. (Photo by David King Gleason)

POULTRY

*Me, I got a frien', an' his name is George Fairchild, who was the very firs'
Jambalaya Festival king. An' he only use ash wood to cook dem jambalaya.
I had to got me some from him an' rat quick 'cause I needed jambalaya
cooked for me an' some of ma good friens'. An' I wanna tol' you somet'ing.
Mr. George can control dat fire aroun' dat washpot better than I can control
the gas on ma stove, I garontee!* (Photo by David King Gleason)

CHICKEN JAMBALAYA

1 large fryer
Salt
Black pepper
Cayenne pepper
1 cup cooking oil
6 medium-sized onions,
   chopped
1 tbsp. bell pepper, chopped
   small

1 tbsp. celery, chopped small
½ lb. hot smoked sausage,
   if desired
3 cups long-grain rice
4 cups water
1 clove garlic, finely chopped

Cut up chicken, wash, and season with salt and both peppers.

Fry until golden brown in cooking oil over hot fire. Lower heat and add all chopped seasonings except garlic. Cook until all seasonings are clear, or onions, bell pepper, and celery are tender.

Here's where you may add the hot sausage. I think this makes a better jambalaya.

Add rice, salt, and pepper to chicken and seasonings. Cook slowly for about 15 minutes over low heat, stirring often. Add the water and chopped garlic, stir, and cover. Do not stir anymore.

Simmer over low flame for about 1 hour, or until rice is done. Keep covered. *Serves 8.*

Variations: This same recipe may be used with pork, duck, squirrel, rabbit, sausage, or beef.

Jambalaya

The original jambalaya was shrimp cooked with rice, and they'd use tomato to give it some color. Chicken is also used now. The secret of a good jambalaya is that every grain of rice is supposed to taste like the meat that's cooked with it.

When they started the Jambalaya Festival in Gonzales, it had to be chicken jambalaya. It gave cooks a chance to show the ways they would brown their chicken. I remember the first Jambalaya Festival king was George Fairchild.

CHICKEN À LA JUSTIN

2 fryers
Salt
Black pepper
Cayenne pepper
Olive oil
4 cups onions, chopped
1 cup shallots or green onions,
    chopped
1 cup bell pepper, chopped

1 cup celery, chopped
2 cups parsley (or 1 cup dried
    parsley), chopped
1 small can pimiento
4 cups Sauterne wine or dry
    white wine
2 tbsp. Worcestershire sauce
Dash Louisiana hot sauce

Preheat oven to 375 degrees.

Cut up chicken as if to fry. Season with salt, black pepper, and cayenne pepper.

Pour olive oil in bottom of baking pan. Arrange chicken in pan. Sprinkle with the chopped onions, bell pepper, celery, and parsley.

Cut pimiento in strips, and place on chicken.

Mix wine, Worcestershire sauce, and dash of hot sauce; pour over chicken.

Bake uncovered until chicken is browned, approximately 1½ to 2 hours. Baste frequently. Add water if needed. *Serves 4-6.*

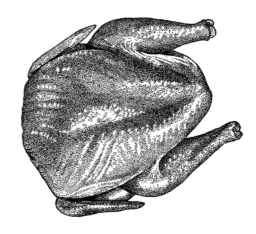

POULET AU GRATIN À LA CASTILLE

2 tbsp. olive oil
1 2-lb. fryer
2 medium-sized onions, chopped
4 medium cloves garlic, chopped
1 cup Sauterne wine or dry white wine
1 can cream of mushroom soup
¼ cup water
1 medium-sized can mushrooms
¼ lb. grated Romano cheese

Cover bottom of skillet with olive oil. Place cut-up chicken in cold olive oil. Brown chicken until almost done. Remove chicken.

In same skillet and oil, brown chopped onions and garlic, then add ¼ cup wine. Put chicken back into skillet, and simmer 15 minutes. Preheat the oven to 325 degrees.

Then place contents of skillet into a casserole. Spoon mushroom soup and water over chicken in casserole, and then add ¾ cup wine. Add can of mushrooms, and sprinkle grated cheese on top.

Bake in the preheated oven until chicken is tender (about 45 minutes). *Serves 6.*

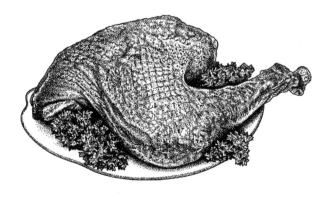

PEACH BRANDY CHICKEN

1 2½-lb. broiler
2 tsp. salt
½ tsp. seasoning salt
1 tsp. Accent
½ tsp. black pepper
2 tbsp. olive oil
1 cup celery, mostly leaves and
   a little stalk, chopped fine

½ cooking apple, sliced
⅓ cup claret wine or dry red
   wine
1 no. 1 can (about 1⅓ cups)
   light syrup peaches, halves
   (drained)
⅓ cup brandy

Cut chicken in half, wash, and pat dry. Rub in salt, seasoning salt, Accent, and pepper.

Put olive oil in cast-iron pot, and brown chicken to golden brown. Arrange rib side down, and add celery and apple. Cook slowly, covered, for 30 minutes. Turn chicken, ribs up, add wine, cover, and cook 15 minutes.

Add peaches, pit side up, and ⅓ cup brandy, pouring some in each peach half and in rib side of chicken. Cover and heat. Take fork and mash gravy with care to get out all lumps, and bring to boil when ready to serve chicken. *Serves 2-4.*

CHICKEN TETRAZZINI

3 tbsp. margarine
2 tbsp. plain flour
½ cup diced green pepper
½ lb. sliced fresh mushrooms
½ cup Sauterne wine or dry
  white wine
1 clove garlic, crushed
2 cups water
1 envelope chunky chicken-
  noodle soup mix

1 broiler or fryer chicken,
  cooked, boned, and cut into
  chunks
1¼ cups grated Parmesan
  cheese
¼ cup chopped parsley
8 oz. uncooked noodles

Melt margarine in a skillet, add flour, and cook until it is brown and the flour taste is gone.

Add green pepper; cook over low heat 4 minutes, stirring frequently. Stir in the mushrooms, and cook until tender. Remove from heat. Blend in the wine and garlic.

Bring water to a boil in a saucepan. Stir in the soup mix. Reduce heat; partially cover and simmer 5 minutes. Add chicken, 1 cup of the cheese, parsley, and vegetable mixtures; heat.

Meanwhile, cook the noodles in boiling, salted water according to the directions on the package. Drain. Arrange noodles in the bottom of a greased 3-quart casserole. Cover with chicken sauce, and stir lightly to mix. Sprinkle with remaining ¼ cup cheese.

Broil until lightly browned on top, about 5 minutes. *Serves 6-8.*

BROILED CHICKEN

Salt
Ground cayenne pepper
3 fryer or broiler chickens,
   halved

½ cup olive oil
1 cup Sauterne wine or dry
   white wine (more if needed)

Rub salt and cayenne pepper well into chicken.

Cover bottom of baking pan with olive oil. Pour in wine, mixing it with the olive oil as much as possible. Wet each side of chicken with this mixture, and place the halves in the pan.

Put under broiler, basting frequently until done. *Serves 6.*

BARBECUED CHICKEN

Beer
Water
1 tsp. or 2 dashes
   Worcestershire sauce to
   each bottle of beer

Halves of broiler or fryer
   chickens
Cooked Barbecue Sauce

Make a basting sauce by mixing half beer and half water and 1 teaspoon or 2 dashes of Worcestershire sauce to each bottle of beer. Make basting sauce as needed.

Place chicken halves on low charcoal fire, turn frequently, and baste both sides before and after turning with the basting sauce.

When chickens are done, finish off with two bastings of Cooked Barbecue Sauce (see my recipe). Put in pan and pour any remaining barbecue sauce over them.

BAKED FRYER

1 3½- to 4-lb. young fryer
Flour
Salt
Pepper
Cooking oil
2 onions, finely chopped
2 green peppers, chopped
1 small garlic clove, minced
1½ tsp. salt
1 tsp. dried mint
½ tsp. cayenne pepper

2 no. 2 cans (about 2½ cups ea.)
    tomatoes
½ tsp. chopped parsley
½ tsp. powdered thyme
2 cups cooked rice
3 heaping tbsp. dried currants
¼ lb. almonds, scalded,
    skinned, and roasted to
    golden brown
Parsley for garnish

Preheat the oven to 325 degrees.

Cut up the chicken in pieces for frying. Remove the skin, and roll pieces in flour, salt, and pepper. Brown in oil. Remove the chicken from the pan, but keep it hot. (This is a secret of the dish's success.)

Into the oil in which the chicken has been browned, put the onions, peppers, and garlic. Cook very slowly, stirring constantly. Season with salt, mint, and cayenne pepper. Add tomatoes, parsley, and thyme.

Put the chicken in a roaster, and pour the mixture over it. If the sauce does not cover the chicken, rinse out the skillet in which the mixture has been cooked, and pour that over the chicken, too. Cover the roaster tightly. Bake in a moderate oven about 45 minutes, until the chicken is tender.

Place the chicken in the center of a large platter. Pile around it the rice, which has been cooked very dry. Drop currants into the sauce, and pour the sauce over the rice. Scatter almonds over the top. Garnish with parsley, and you have food for the gods. *Serves 6-8.*

BAKED CHICKEN ON A SUNDAY COOKED ON A TUESDAY À LA WALTER GUITREAU

1 2- to 3-lb. chicken
1 can cream of celery soup
1 can cream of mushroom
  soup

2 soup cans milk
2 cups uncooked rice
1 envelope dried onion soup
  mix

Preheat the oven to 325 degrees.

Skin and cut up the chicken into chunks. Pour the celery soup, mushroom soup, and milk over the rice, and mix well. Pour the rice mixture into a 9-by-12-inch greased baking pan. Place the chicken on top, and sprinkle the onion soup over the whole mess. Cover with aluminum foil.

Bake in the preheated oven for 2 to 2½ hours. Just put it in there and forget about it. Bake until the chicken falls off the bone. *Serves 6.*

"It was Walter's turn to cook for the bourré players while dey lose all our money. He called his dish Baked Chicken on a Sunday. But he made it on a Tuesday. It ain't not'ing in the world but baked jambalaya. An' it's delicious."

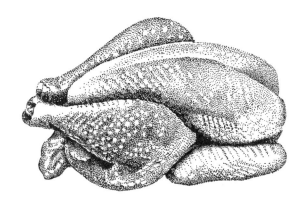

Yorkshire Chicken

1¼ cups flour
3 tsp. salt
1 tsp. ground sage
¼ tsp. cayenne pepper
2½ to 3 lb. chicken pieces,
   for frying
¼ cup oil

1 tsp. baking powder
3 eggs, well beaten
1½ cups milk
¼ cup melted butter
   or margarine
¼ cup chopped parsley

Preheat the oven to 350 degrees.

Combine ¼ cup flour, 2 tsp. salt, the sage, and pepper in a bag. Add chicken, and shake, coating pieces evenly. Brown the chicken in oil on all sides in a large skillet. Remove to a deep 2-quart casserole.

Sift the remaining 1 cup flour, the remaining teaspoon of salt, and baking powder.

Combine the eggs, milk, melted butter, and parsley. Blend with the flour mixture until smooth. Pour over chicken.

Bake in the preheated oven for 1 hour or until done. *Serves 4.*

Special Oven-Fried Turkey

1 fryer-roaster turkey, 4 to 6 lb.
   ready-to-cook weight, cut
   into serving pieces
Salt and cayenne pepper
1¼ cups melted butter or
   margarine

¼ tsp. bitters (Peychaud or
   Angostura)
2 cups seasoned bread crumbs

Preheat the oven to 350 degrees.

Season turkey pieces with salt and cayenne pepper. Dip in butter and bitters, then roll in crumbs. Place pieces, skin side up (not touching), in a greased baking pan. Drizzle with half of the remaining butter, and sprinkle with remaining crumbs. Cover the pan with aluminum foil.

Bake in the preheated oven for 1 hour. Uncover, and pour remaining butter over turkey. Bake, uncovered, for 30 to 45 minutes longer, or until the meat is tender and brown. *Serves 6-8.*

Sweet 'N' Sour Turkey Wings

6 turkey wings
2 cups water
1 rib celery
1 tsp. salt
¼ tsp. pepper
2 tbsp. plain flour
3 tbsp. olive oil
1½ cups chicken or turkey
   stock

½ cup vinegar
⅓ cup soy sauce
⅓ cup catsup or chili sauce
1 cup roll-cut carrots
1 cup green pepper, cut into
   strips
1 cup drained pineapple
   chunks

Separate the turkey wings at the joints, and discard tips. Wash, drain, and cook in water along with celery, salt, and pepper. Simmer, covered, over low heat until tender.

Meanwhile, brown the flour in 1 tablespoon of the olive oil in a small saucepan. Add stock, vinegar, soy sauce, and catsup; cook and stir until thick. Set aside.

Heat a large skillet, and add the remaining 2 tablespoons of the olive oil. Fry carrots for 1 minute, stirring constantly. Add green pepper and pineapple, and heat.

Blend together the sweet 'n' sour sauce and tender wing pieces. Bring to a simmer. Serve hot over rice. *Serves 6.*

SEAFOOD

Mos' everyone gonna agree: They is shrimp, an' they is shrimp, an' they is shrimp. An' then they is Gulf shrimp! (Photo by Bill Cooksey)

Boiled Shrimp in Shell

4 qt. water (enough to cover shrimp)
8 lemons, quartered
3 large onions, quartered
2 cloves garlic, coarsely chopped
1 stalk celery, coarsely chopped

3 cups Sauterne wine or dry white wine
2 tbsp. Worcestershire sauce
Salt
2 tbsp. ground cayenne pepper
5 lb. shrimp, raw

Put water in pot large enough to hold shrimp and all the seasonings, and place it on a hot fire.

Drop into the water the lemons, onions, garlic, and celery. Add wine and Worcestershire sauce. Add salt until liquid is too salty for your taste. Add the pepper. Bring to a boil, and then add the shrimp.

Cook 20 minutes or so, depending on the size of the shrimp. Watch the shrimp, and when the hull stands away from the meat, they are done. Another way to tell is that they usually float. The best way to determine whether the shrimp are done is to taste them after 15 or 20 minutes of boiling.

Pour juice off shrimp, and let them steam for 15 minutes. Then place on a large tray and cool. *Serves 4-6.*

Variation: Substitute 2 or 3 dozen crabs for shrimp. Add more salt, since crabs and other shellfish require more salt than do shrimp.

"Jus' peel an' eat them shrimp. You don' need no sauce, 'cause they delicious jus' as they is. While they is cookin', pick one up ever' now an' then an' taste it to see if it done. I can't never wait more'n about 5 or 4 minutes to try this, myself."

DRESSING FOR BOILED SHRIMP

4 heaping tbsp. mayonnaise
2 tbsp. olive oil
2 tsp. Louisiana hot sauce
1 large bottle (16 oz.) catsup
1 tsp. salt

1 tbsp. Worcestershire sauce
Juice from 1 whole lemon
1 level tbsp. prepared
　　creamed-style horseradish

Place mayonnaise in bowl, add olive oil slowly, beating constantly, with fork. Beat mayonnaise back to original firmness.

Add Louisiana hot sauce, then add catsup, beating all the while. Add salt and Worcestershire sauce.

Squeeze lemon into catsup bottle, getting remains of catsup. Pour into mixture, add horseradish, cover and chill for about 30 minutes. Beat just before serving.

Additional horseradish may be added to individual servings, if desired. *Serves 8.*

SHRIMP MOLD

1 can condensed tomato soup
1 large pkg. cream cheese
2 pkg. unflavored gelatin
½ cup water
1 cup mayonnaise

4 or 5 green onions
Salt
Pepper
Louisiana hot sauce
2 cups boiled shrimp, chopped

Heat the soup to a boil. Stir in cream cheese.

Dissolve gelatin in ½ cup water, and add to the soup mix. Let cool. Add all other ingredients (except shrimp).

Arrange the mold in layers of sauce and shrimp. Chill until mold is set. *Serves 6-8.*

SHRIMP À LA MEXICANA

2 tsp. cooking oil
1 medium onion, chopped
½ cup chopped bell pepper
½ cup chopped celery
1 6-oz. can whole, peeled
 tomatoes
3 cloves garlic, minced, or
 garlic powder to taste
½ tsp. cayenne pepper

Salt to taste
1 tsp. paprika
½ cup Sauterne wine or dry
 white wine
1 tbsp. flour
1 lb. cooked shrimp
Cooked rice
1 cup grated cheddar cheese

Sauté the onion, bell pepper, and celery in heated oil. Add the tomatoes, garlic, pepper, salt, paprika, wine, and flour. Blend well, and simmer for 45 minutes.

Add cooked shrimp, and simmer for 15 minutes.

Serve over rice, and top with grated cheese. *Serves 6-8.*

SHRIMP À LA CREOLE

3 tbsp. olive oil
½ cup onion, chopped
½ cup celery, chopped
½ cup parsley, chopped
⅓ cup bell pepper, chopped
2 cups water
2 cups tomatoes
1 cup tomato sauce

1 small clove garlic, minced
½ tsp. Worcestershire sauce
½ tsp. Louisiana hot sauce
 (cayenne)
1 tsp. salt
1 lb. raw shrimp, deveined
3 cups cooked rice

Sauté onion, celery, parsley, and bell pepper in olive oil until tender. Add water, tomatoes, tomato sauce, and garlic. Simmer 5 minutes, then add Worcestershire sauce, Louisiana hot sauce, and salt.

Cook mixture for 30 minutes. Add shrimp, and cook for 30 more minutes, or until shrimp are done and mixture is thick.

Serve over rice. *Serves 4.*

Mirliton Stuffed with Shrimp

STUFFING

6 medium-sized mirlitons
3 tbsp. margarine
²⁄₃ cup finely chopped onion
3 slices bread, soaked in water
   and squeezed
¼ cup shallots

¼ cup chopped parsley
1 tsp. salt
¼ tsp. cayenne pepper
2 cups medium shrimp, peeled
   and deveined
Olive oil

Preheat the oven to 350 degrees.

Cut mirlitons in half lengthwise, and place in a pot of boiling water. Cover, and boil for 15 minutes or until tender.

Remove seeds, and scoop out the pulp. Keep pulp and shells.

Sauté the onions in margarine for 5 minutes. Add mirliton pulp, bread, shallots, parsley, salt, and pepper. Continue cooking for approximately 10 minutes. Mix well, stirring constantly. Add shrimp.

Pile the mixture into mirliton shells, and place stuffed mirlitons in a baking pan with about ⅛ inch of olive oil.

TOPPING

3 tbsp. melted margarine   ¼ cup plain bread crumbs

Top the stuffed shells with buttered bread crumbs, and bake 30 minutes in the preheated oven. *Serves 6-8.*

BROILED SHRIMP À LA JUSTIN

¼ cup olive oil
1 stick butter or margarine
2 tsp. Worcestershire sauce
1 tsp. Louisiana red hot sauce
3 lb. raw peeled shrimp

Salt
Ground cayenne pepper
1 cup Sauterne wine or dry
   white wine

Preheat the oven to 350 degrees.

Put olive oil in bottom of baking pan, and chip butter into it. Place in oven until butter is melted. Then take pan out and add Worcestershire sauce and hot sauce. Mix well.

Place shrimp in single layer into the mixture, and salt and pepper them.

Pour wine into pan, using approximately 1 cup or as much as is needed to half cover the shrimp.

Bake in the preheated oven for 20 minutes. Then place in broiler until shrimp begin to brown. Baste frequently. *Serves 6-8.*

"Them broiled shrimp is a little bit tricky. Don' you broil them too long, an' not too fast, an' they will be good, I garontee.

"One time I slip up a little an' broil them too long. They did not taste too good, but they sure made nice new half-soles for my shoes!"

FRENCH-FRIED SHRIMP

2 large onions, sliced
1 clove garlic
1 bell pepper, sliced
3 lb. shrimp, deveined
4 eggs
1 cup Sauterne wine or dry
   white wine

1 tbsp. Worcestershire sauce
1 tsp. Louisiana hot sauce
1 cup Parmesan cheese
Milk
Salt to taste
Pancake flour

Put sliced onions, garlic, and bell pepper in a blender and process. Place shrimp in large bowl and add onions, garlic, and bell pepper.

In another bowl, beat 4 eggs, adding Sauterne wine slowly while beating.

Pour this over shrimp, adding Worcestershire sauce and hot sauce. Add in the cheese. Stir this mixture well. Add milk to cover shrimp. Stir until milk mixes well. Salt to taste. Marinate overnight.

To fry shrimp, place pancake flour (as much as needed) in brown paper sack and add a little salt. Drain shrimp a few at a time, and shake in pancake flour. Fry in deep fat until golden brown. *Serves 4-6.*

"If you like to eat jus' a little bit, I think this is the mos' delicious fried shrimp recipe I done ever taste.

"If you can possibly marinate them shrimp about 12 hours, or maybe overnight, they gonna soak up all that juices an' taste even better."

SHRIMP IN GREEN SAUCE OVER RICE

1½ lb. raw shrimp, shelled and
  deveined
¼ cup butter or margarine
⅓ cup finely minced onion
3 tbsp. flour
2½ cups chicken broth
½ cup Sauterne wine or dry
  white wine

½ cup minced parsley
Pinch cayenne pepper
½ cup sliced stuffed olives
¼ tsp. bitters (Peychaud or
  Angostura)
2 tsp. soy sauce
6 cups hot cooked rice

Cook the shrimp in boiling, salted water until pink (about 4 minutes). Drain and set aside.

Melt the butter in a heavy saucepan, add onions, and cook until soft, but not browned. Blend in flour.

Gradually add chicken broth and wine; cook, stirring constantly, until the sauce thickens. Add parsley, cayenne pepper, olives, bitters, soy sauce, and shrimp. Simmer until thoroughly heated.

Serve over beds of hot rice. *Serves 6.*

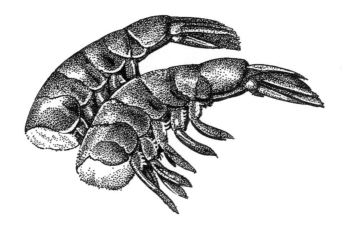

SHRIMP STEW

½ cup olive oil
1 cup flour
4 medium onions, chopped
½ cup chopped bell pepper
½ cup chopped celery
1 clove garlic, finely chopped
1 cup parsley, chopped,
   or ½ cup dried parsley

3 lb. shrimp, peeled and
   deveined
Salt
Cayenne pepper
3 cups water
Cooked rice

Using an iron pot, if possible, heat the oil, add flour, and cook to a dark brown over a low fire. Be sure to keep stirring this mixture constantly. If the phone rings, don't answer.

Add chopped seasonings, and simmer over low heat about 1 hour.

Season the shrimp with salt and pepper, and add to the sauce. Cover and simmer together for about ½ hour. Keep the heat low.

Add 3 cups water, cover, and continue to simmer over low heat for about 1 more hour.

Serve over rice. *Serves 6-8.*

CRAWFISH CASSEROLE

½ cup crawfish fat (if you
    don't have it, use ¼ cup
    margarine)
1 cup celery, diced
1½ cups onion, chopped
⅓ cup green bell pepper,
    chopped
½ cup green-onion tops,
    chopped
1 10½-oz. can cream of
    mushroom soup

2 small cloves garlic, chopped
6 sprigs parsley, chopped
2 cups crawfish tails
3 slices moistened bread
2 cups cooked rice
½ cup Sauterne wine or dry
    white wine
1 cup water
¼ cup margarine
Bread crumbs
Paprika

Preheat the oven to 375 degrees.

Sauté celery, onions, and bell pepper in crawfish fat (or margarine) until tender. Add green-onion tops, soup, garlic, parsley, and crawfish tails. Heat slowly until hot. Add bread, rice, wine, and water and cook 15 minutes longer. Season to taste.

Turn the mixture into a 2-quart casserole dish. Dot with margarine; sprinkle with bread crumbs and paprika.

Cover and bake in the preheated oven for 30 minutes. *Serves 8.*

Crawfish (pronounced kraw-fish)

Those little crawfish that taste so good boiled or cooked up as étouffée and other wondermous dishes are just that—crawfish. Not crayfish. Not crawdads. It makes me mad when people call them anything other than crawfish! And of course, South Louisiana cooks prefer to use the home-grown variety over the ones imported from China. They just taste better!

Dis is me an' ma good frien, Les Brown. An' I wanna tol' you, he is a good crawfish people. He caught dem crawfish for me an' he loves to did dat.
(Photo by David King Gleason)

CRAWFISH ETOUFFÉE

1 lb. margarine (use crawfish
   fat if you have it)
5½ lb. chopped onion
4 cups chopped bell pepper
4 cups parsley
1 tbsp. Louisiana hot sauce
2 tbsp. Worcestershire sauce

4 tsp. salt to taste (don't add
   all at one time; taste, then
   add)
2 tbsp. lemon juice
5 to 6 lb. crawfish tails

Put margarine or crawfish fat in a pan. Add chopped onions, bell pepper, parsley, Louisiana hot sauce, and Worcestershire sauce. Season with salt and lemon juice.

Simmer, covered, for an hour. (This will make its own juice.)

Then add the crawfish and cook, covered, for 30 minutes to an hour. *Serves 6-8.*

CRAWFISH STEW

½ cup olive oil
1 cup flour
4 medium onions, chopped
½ cup bell pepper, chopped
½ cup celery, chopped
1 cup parsley, chopped,
   or ½ cup dried parsley
1 clove garlic, chopped

3 lb. crawfish tails, cleaned
   and deveined
Salt
Black pepper
Cayenne pepper
3 cups water
Cooked rice

Heat oil in a cast-iron pot, if possible, then add flour, and brown to a dark brown over a low fire. Be certain to keep stirring this mixture constantly. If the phone rings, don't answer.

Add chopped seasonings, simmer over low heat about 1 hour. Season crawfish tails with salt, black, and cayenne pepper and add to sauce.

Cover and simmer for about ½ hour on low heat. Add 3 cups of water, cover, and continue to simmer over low heat for about 1 more hour.

Serve over rice. *Serves 6-8.*

CRAWFISH SAUCE PIQUANTE

1 cup olive oil
2 cups flour
26 oz. onions, chopped
10 oz. bell pepper, chopped
8 oz. celery, chopped
6 oz. green onions, chopped
7½-8 oz. parsley, chopped
2½ qt. water

2 8-oz. cans tomato sauce
1 tbsp. finely chopped garlic
1 cup Sauterne wine or dry
   white wine
½ cup Louisiana hot sauce
½ cup Worcestershire sauce
3 tbsp. salt
6 lb. crawfish

Make a dark roux with the olive oil and flour. Add onion, bell pepper, and celery. Cook until the vegetables are clear. Add green onions and parsley, and cook until juiced. Stir in the water, tomato sauce, garlic, wine, hot sauce, Worcestershire sauce, and salt.

If there is no fat on the crawfish, you should add ¼ pound margarine. Add the crawfish. Bring to a boil, and let simmer for about 2 hours. *Serves about 12.*

BARBECUED OYSTERS

½ cup chili powder
½ cup plain flour
1 tsp. cayenne pepper
1 tsp. garlic powder

1 tbsp. salt
1 tsp. hickory-smoked salt
4 doz. oysters
Cooking oil

Put the dry ingredients in a heavy paper bag and shake real well. Add oysters, one at a time, and shake.

Deep fry in hot fat (360 to 365 degrees) until done. *Serves 4-6.*

BAKED AND BROILED OYSTERS

**Large oysters, as many as you
    want**
Nonstick cooking spray

Seasoned salt
Lemon-pepper seasoning
Worcestershire sauce

Preheat the oven to 250 degrees.

Drain the oysters well, spray a baking pan with cooking spray, and place one layer of oysters in it.

Sprinkle with seasoned salt and lemon-pepper seasoning. Dash Worcestershire sauce on each oyster.

Bake at 250 degrees for 15 to 20 minutes, then broil until brown.

BROILED OYSTERS

Nonstick cooking spray
Salt
Butter-flavored salt
Lemon-pepper seasoning

**Sauterne wine or
    dry white wine**
Large oysters

Spray a baking pan with cooking spray. Sprinkle salt, butter-flavored salt, and lemon pepper over each oyster.

Pour a little wine in the bottom of the pan to use for basting.

Add oysters, and broil until done. Eat as soon as they come out of the oven.

Only 8½ pound of them crab? Hell, me, I could eat all that many by mah-self, I garontee! (Photo by Bill Cooksey)

BARBECUED CRABS

½ cup chili powder
½ cup plain flour
1 tsp. ground cayenne pepper
1 tsp. garlic powder

1 tbsp. salt
1 tsp. hickory-smoked salt
6 crab bodies
Cooking oil

Put the dry ingredients in a heavy paper bag, and shake to mix. Add crab bodies one at a time and shake.

Fry crabs in deep, hot fat (about 160 to 365 degrees) until done. *Serves 4-6.*

Alma Picou, she say she catch them catfish if me, I'll cook them. An' I will, too! (Photo by Bill Cooksey)

FRIED CATFISH

10 lb. catfish
1 cup milk
2½ cups cornmeal
Ground cayenne pepper
1 tsp. butter-flavored salt

1 cup plain flour
Salt
1 tsp. garlic powder
Cooking oil

Soak catfish in milk.

Mix the dry ingredients thoroughly in a bowl or bag.

Roll the fish in dry ingredients.

Fry in hot cooking oil deep enough to float the fish. (Be sure grease or oil is not too hot.) *Serves 8-10.*

Dose catfish what Murphy Brown hold up dare for me, dey jus' the good eatin' size. You can filet dem if you want, an' you can steak dem if you want. An' I axed Murphy where he got dose. An' he tol' me, an' I believe him also, too. (Photo by David King Gleason)

CATFISH MANCHAC À LA WALTER AND JUSTIN

Catfish	Garlic powder
Louisiana hot sauce	Chili powder
Self-rising flour	Onion powder
Seasoned cornmeal	Lemon-pepper seasoning
Salt	2 eggs
Cayenne pepper	1 qt. milk

Slice the catfish thin when it is half-thawed. Marinate for 2-3 hours in Louisiana hot sauce. Drain.

Mix together equal parts of flour and cornmeal. Season that mixture with salt, cayenne pepper, garlic powder, chili powder, onion powder, lemon-pepper seasoning, and anything else you want to throw in there.

Mix together the eggs and milk.

Dip the fish in the milk mixture, then in the dry mix. (Be sure the fish is completely thawed before dipping.)

Deep fry at about 365 degrees until fish floats to the top. Bread only as needed, right before frying.

Walter Guitreau caught dis forty-fo'-poun' catfish an' mos' fell overboard to got him in de boat. We made courtbouillon wit' de head, an serv' dat wit' rice, an' tol' ma grandson dat it was fish heads an' rice. An' dat's what it was, yeah! (Photo by David King Gleason)

CATFISH COURTBOUILLON (COO-BEE-YON)

½ cup olive oil
1 cup flour
8 medium onions, chopped
4 cups green onions, chopped
1 cup celery, chopped
½ cup bell pepper, chopped
1 clove garlic, chopped
½ cup parsley, chopped,
   or ¼ cup dried parsley

1 3- to 6- lb. large catfish
Salt
Black pepper
Cayenne pepper
2 cups water
Cooked rice

Heat the oil. Add flour, and brown. Add chopped seasonings. Simmer 1 hour.

Cut up fish in large pieces. Season with salt and both peppers. Add to the above sauce. Add water.

Cover and cook over low heat about 1 hour. Serve over rice. *Serves 6-8.*

That ol' Mississippi is a plumb good place for me to do my contemplate, I garontee! (Photo by Bill Cooksey)

FISH COURTBOUILLON À LA JUSTIN

2 tbsp. olive oil
3 cups onion, chopped
2 cups celery, chopped
1 cup bell pepper, chopped
½ cup parsley, chopped
2 cups green onions, chopped
1 tbsp. garlic, chopped
2 cups grated carrots
5 or 6 cups fish, boned
   and skinned

¼ cup chopped lemon
2 cups Sauterne wine or dry
   white wine
8 cups water
1 tbsp. soy sauce
1 tbsp. Worcestershire sauce
2 tsp. Louisiana hot sauce
¼ tsp. bitters (Peychaud
   or Angostura)
3 to 4 tsp. salt

Sauté or simmer the onions, celery, and bell pepper in olive oil until clear.

Add parsley, green onions, garlic, and carrots, and simmer for about 15 minutes.

Add the fish, lemon, wine, and the remainder of the ingredients.

Bring to a boil, and let cook over low heat (nearly simmer) for 3-4 hours. Do not stir. This can be made with a light roux, too. *Serves 6-8.*

Me, I know how to catch them and also, too, how to clean them. (Photo by David King Gleason)

BROILED FLOUNDER

1 bunch green onions, finely
 diced
1 large clove garlic, finely
 diced
Olive oil
Salt

Cayenne pepper
4 medium-sized dressed
 flounder
2 cups Sauterne wine or dry
 white wine

Sauté onions and garlic in enough olive oil to cover the bottom of a saucepan.

Cover the bottom of a large baking pan with olive oil about ⅛-inch deep.

Salt and pepper the flounder, and place in the pan.

Pour wine into pan, being careful not to wash the salt and pepper off the fish.

Spread sautéed onions and garlic over the flounder. Broil until done. (It might be wise to bake the fish in a 350-degree oven for about 10 or 15 minutes before putting it under the broiler.) *Serves 4-6.*

BROILED RED SNAPPER

1 6- to 8-lb. red snapper
3 sticks butter or margarine
Juice from 2 lemons
1 tbsp. Worcestershire sauce

2 tbsp. olive oil
1 tsp. salt
½ tsp. Louisiana hot sauce

Place the red snapper in a greased pan.

Broil for 15-25 minutes.

Heat the butter, lemon juice, Worcestershire sauce, olive oil, salt, and hot sauce in a pan. Never bring to a boil.

Pour over the fish when served. *Serves 8.*

Sometime when the weather is real bad, it's best to use a silver hook to caught dem fish like I'm doin' right here, instead of goin' out dare an' tryin' to caught dem in the river. An' I know dat ol' Murphy Brown is not goin' to sold me some fish dat are not so good, no. (Photo by David King Gleason)

BAKED RED SNAPPER

1 6- to 10-lb. large red snapper	Salt
Olive oil for sautéing	Ground cayenne pepper
2½ cups chopped green onions	2 tbsp. dried parsley flakes
1 rib chopped celery	3 cups Sauterne wine or dry
2 13-oz. cans mushrooms,	white wine
stems and pieces	4 dashes wine vinegar
¼ cup olive oil	1 tbsp. Worcestershire sauce

Preheat the oven to 375 degrees.

Sauté onions, celery, and mushrooms in a frying pan in a little olive oil.

Pour ¼ cup olive oil in baking pan. Salt and pepper the fish to taste, and place it in the pan. Spread sautéed onions, celery, and mushrooms over the fish. Now sprinkle the parsley on top of the other ingredients.

Rinse frying pan (used for sautéing) with the wine, and pour over fish. Add vinegar and Worcestershire sauce.

Bake in the preheated oven, basting occasionally, until fish is cooked. *Serves 8-10.*

"When you stick a fork in this fish and it comes out with a little bits of fish clingin' to it, this is did, for sure. It become flaky when it is did.

"An' that's when you start snappin' at each other when you eat it. That's why they name it red snapper, I guess.

"You mus' watch this fish broilin' quite a bit, an' baste it with them juices, which are jus' wondermous. I even know me some people what t'row them fishes away an' just sop up the juice.

"Ooh, boy! What a big lie that was!

"Oh, yes, if you use froze' fish, be dam' sure to thaw it plumb out before you cooks it. An' that's a order!"

GARFISH BALLS

2 onions	2 cups flour
6 cups ground garfish (see below for instructions)	Water
	1 8-oz. can tomato sauce
1 potato	½ cup tomato catsup
1 red pepper	1 bell pepper, chopped
4 eggs, beaten	Onion tops, chopped
Salt and pepper to taste	Parsley
1 cup olive oil	

Grind one onion for the roux, and set aside.

Grind the garfish, one onion, potato, and red pepper. (Scrape the fish from the skin and bone before grinding, using a spoon.) Mix well, then add the eggs, and salt and pepper to taste.

Form mixture into balls. (Wet your hands occasionally so the fish won't stick to your hands.) Fry the balls until brown.

Make a roux with the olive oil and flour. Add water, tomato sauce, tomato catsup, and bell pepper. Let simmer for 1 hour.

Add fishballs, onion tops, and parsley, and cook another hour. Serve hot. *Serves 6-10.*

"I'll never forgot dat firs' batch we made, no. Ooh boy! Dey was so hard, nobody would eat 'em! Not even the dogs would touch 'em! But dey did make good golf balls, I garontee!"

Hoo, boy! How can anything that taste so good look so bad? Huh? Me and Buddy Gregoire are admirin' one ornery turtle. (Photo by Bill Cooksey)

TURTLE ETOUFFÉE

10 lb. turtle meat, cleaned
Salt and pepper
Olive oil
8 large onions, chopped well
3 bell peppers, chopped well
1 clove garlic, finely chopped

Juice from ½ lemon
1 cup of parsley, chopped,
    or ½ cup dried parsley
1 tbsp. Worcestershire sauce
Cooked rice

Wash and drain turtle meat. Salt and pepper meat, and brown it in olive oil.

Put in a heavy pot, and add all other ingredients.

Cook on low heat for 6-8 hours, until turtle meat is tender.

Serve with rice. *Serves 6-10.*

Note: The only juice in the turtle étouffée is the natural juice of the vegetable ingredients. Do not add water, wine, or any other juice.

GAME

You can tell by the look on my face that I got him! (Photo by David King Gleason)

Baked Goose

1 domestic or wild goose
Vinegar
Water
Salt
Ground cayenne pepper
1 turnip, peeled whole
½-¾ cup olive oil
1 cup flour
2 large onions, chopped
½ cup parsley, chopped

3 cups water
2 cloves garlic, minced
3 cups Sauterne wine or dry
   white wine
1 can cream of mushroom
   soup
Juice from 1 lemon
1 tbsp. Worcestershire sauce
1 small bay leaf

If the goose is wild, marinate in ¼ vinegar and ¾ water to cover goose for 4-12 hours. If goose is domestic, marinate for 1-3 hours.

Remove goose from marinade, and wash really well with cold water. Drain well.

Preheat the oven to 375 degrees.

Salt and pepper the goose. Place turnip inside goose.

In roasting pan, brown flour slowly, over low fire, in olive oil until brown. Add onions and parsley. Stir for 2 or 3 minutes. Add water, garlic, wine, mushroom soup, lemon juice, Worcestershire sauce, and bay leaf (on toothpick to be removed after 1 hour of cooking).

Place goose on rack and place in roaster, cover and baste occasionally. Add water if necessary. Add salt and pepper to gravy if needed.

Bake in the preheated oven 2 hours and remove cover to brown if needed. *Serves 4-6.*

PHEASANT AU VIN

2 large pheasants, whole
Water
Wine vinegar
Salt
1 tsp. salt
Ground cayenne pepper

Olive oil
2 8-oz. cans cream
  of mushroom soup
1 bay leaf
2 cups Sauterne wine or dry
  white wine

Wash birds well, and let them drain.

Marinate for about an hour in an equal mixture of water and wine vinegar, with a little salt.

Preheat the oven to 200 degrees.

Remove birds from marinade, rinse lightly, and drain. Salt and pepper them well, rubbing the seasonings into the birds.

Cover bottom of baking pan with olive oil. Place pheasants in baking pan. Add cream of mushroom soup and bay leaf.

Cover pan, and place in the preheated, slow oven for 30 minutes.

Add wine, and then cook for about 2 more hours or until meat is done. Baste about every 15 to 20 minutes. The last few minutes of baking may be done with the cover off for browning. *Serves 4-6.*

"This recipe works jus' fine with any fowl that cooks dry."

BROILED QUAIL

6 quail   ½ lemon
Salt   Buttered toast
Ground cayenne pepper   Sautéed mushrooms
Olive oil
½ cup Sauterne wine or dry
   white wine

Split dressed birds down the back. Salt and pepper them, rubbing seasonings well into birds.

Cover bottom of broiling pan with olive oil, about ⅛-inch deep, and rub sides of pan with oil also. Add ½ cup Sauterne.

Place birds in pan, and place 3 inches away from flame in pre-heated broiler for 8-10 minutes, basting frequently.

Turn and broil on other side for same amount of time, basting again. Squeeze lemon over quail about 5 minutes before removing from broiler.

Serve on buttered toast, surrounded by sautéed mushrooms. *Serves 4-6.*

Doves or Quail in Wine Sauce
(Very Good!)

15 doves or quail
Salt and pepper to taste
2 cups of flour
1½ cups cooking oil
2 large onions, very finely
   chopped
Celery to equal the same
   amount as onions, also very
   finely chopped

2 cups Sauterne wine or dry
   white wine
2 cups water
½ stick butter or margarine,
   cut into squares
3 bay leaves

Preheat the oven to 375 degrees.

Salt and pepper doves or quail, dust with flour, and brown in cooking oil.

Place doves in large ovenware casserole, and sprinkle onions and celery over the game. Pour wine and water over this. Dot with butter, and stick bay leaves with toothpicks so they can be readily removed. Place bay leaves, with toothpicks, in the game.

Cover casserole tightly, and bake in the preheated oven until onions and celery are almost clear, approximately 2 hours. Baste occasionally. This gravy is very good over rice. *Serves 8-15.*

Barbecued Duck (Wild or Domestic)

3-6 ducks
1 cup vinegar
Sauterne wine or dry white
  wine
Water
Small onions

Small potatoes or turnips
Garlic cloves
Olive oil
Salt
Cayenne pepper

Wash duck carcasses carefully, then place in deep pan and cover with vinegar and an equal mixture of wine and water. Let ducks soak 2 hours, then drain.

Insert in each duck 1 small onion, 1 small potato or turnip, and ½ small clove of garlic.

Place ¼-inch olive oil in bottom of deep pan. Heat over charcoal fire in hooded barbecue pit. Then add ducks, after salt and cayenne pepper have been sprinkled generously on them. Sear ducks on all sides in olive oil.

Add 1½ cups wine in bottom of pan. Baste well. In 10 minutes, add ½ cup water and ½ cup wine. Baste frequently until ducks are done. Add more wine and water mixture, if needed. *Serves 6-8.*

*You see dat duck on dat island dare? Dat would make real good duck an'
turnip. Oooh, boy! But you know somet'ing? Sara would have killed* me *if
I'd killed dat duck!* (Photo by David King Gleason)

WILD DUCKS AND TURNIPS

4-6 wild ducks
6-8 cups chopped turnips
1 cup cooking oil
1 cup flour
3 cups chopped onion
1 cup celery, chopped
1 cup sweet bell pepper,
   chopped
4-6 cups water
3 cups Sauterne wine or dry
   white wine

1 tbsp. minced garlic
1 cup chopped green onion
1 cup parsley
1 tbsp. Worcestershire sauce
1 tbsp. soy sauce
½ tsp. bitters (Peychaud or
   Angostura)
2 tsp. Louisiana hot sauce
Salt to taste

Brown the ducks, and put them in a pot big enough to cook the whole meal.

Arrange turnips around the ducks.

Make a roux with the oil and flour. Stir in chopped onions, celery, and sweet bell pepper, and cook until the vegetables are clear.

Then add 4 to 6 cups of water, the wine, and the other ingredients.
Pour this over the ducks and turnips.

Cook 4-6 hours on low heat. *Serves 6-8.*

"I need to tol' you somet'ing here. Don' you try an' use live decoys to caught dem duck. You would have a helluva time tryin' to teach live decoys to play dead! But when you caught dem duck, you can make you some fine duck an' turnip.

"An' I wanna tol' you somet'ing else, too, also.

"I know people who will quit their jobs to eat dis. Like dis fella from Lafayette. I tol' him I'm fixin' to cook duck an' turnip. He say, "Forget about what I'm doin' here, I'm on my way rat now."

"An' he come on down rat here to eat dose duck."

Les' see dare, now. I can't make up ma head whether we're gonna serv' dis rabbit sauce piquante wit' spaghetti or wit' rice. Dey are both some wondermous, I garontee! (Photo by David King Gleason)

RABBIT SAUCE PIQUANTE

4 lb. rabbit, cut into 2-inch cubes
Salt
Black pepper
Cayenne pepper
¾ cup bacon drippings
1 cup olive oil
1 cup all-purpose flour
2 8-oz. cans tomato sauce
8 medium onions, chopped
2 bunches green onions,
  chopped

1 large bell pepper, chopped
1 cup celery, chopped
6 cups water
2 cloves garlic, chopped
2 tbsp. Worcestershire sauce
Juice from 2 lemons
¼ tsp. bitters (Peychaud
  or Angostura)
2 cups Sauterne wine or dry
  white wine

Wash the rabbit, season with salt and pepper, and fry in bacon drippings until brown. Remove meat from fat, and set aside.

Make a roux, using the olive oil, flour, and tomato sauce (see my roux recipe).

Add all the chopped seasonings except garlic, cover, and simmer on low heat for about 1 hour.

Add the rabbit to the roux and chopped seasonings mixture, and simmer for 30 minutes, covered.

Stir in water, garlic, Worcestershire sauce, lemon juice, bitters, and wine; cover; and let cook slowly for about 2 or more hours.

Serve over rice or spaghetti. *Serves 8-10.*

RABBIT ETOUFFÉE

1 cup olive oil
1 domestic or wild rabbit, cut up
3 cups onion, chopped
1 cup celery, chopped
1 cup bell pepper, chopped
½ cup parsley, chopped
1 tbsp. garlic, chopped

2 tbsp. Worcestershire sauce
1 tsp. Louisiana hot sauce
2 cups Sauterne wine or dry
  white wine
Salt
Ground cayenne pepper

In a Dutch oven, brown the rabbit in olive oil.

Add all of the other ingredients. Salt and pepper to taste.

Cover, and cook over low heat for 2 hours. *Serves 3-6.*

SQUIRREL STEW

½ cup bacon drippings
¾ cup flour
2 cups onions, chopped
1½ cups celery, chopped
1 cup bell pepper, chopped
1 cup green onions, chopped
½ cup parsley, chopped,
   or ¼ cup dried parsley
2 cups water

1 cup Sauterne wine or dry
   white wine
1 tsp. Louisiana hot sauce
Dash bitters (Peychaud or
   Angostura)
2 cloves garlic, chopped
1 tbsp. soy sauce
3-4 squirrels
2 tsp. salt and pepper to taste

Some people like to brown the squirrel before they cook it. Either way, first you make a roux with the bacon drippings and the flour. Get it as dark as you like it, which should be pretty dark.

Cook the onions, celery, and bell peppers until clear. Add green onions and parsley. Add the water, wine, hot sauce, bitters, garlic, and soy sauce.

Add the squirrels and cook a few hours or so over a low fire. Season with salt and pepper to taste. *Serves 4-6.*

BROILED SQUIRREL

3 squirrels with heads
   removed
Vinegar and water
Salt

Ground cayenne pepper
¼ cup olive oil
1 cup claret, Sauterne wine, or
   dry white wine

Marinate squirrels in mixture of vinegar and water, ¼ vinegar to ¾ water, for a minimum of 3 hours, preferably longer, up to 24 hours.

After marinating, wash squirrels with cold water. Salt and pepper them.

Grease pan with some of the olive oil, and pour the rest over squirrels after they are placed in pan. Add wine. Broil until done, basting often. *Serves 4-6.*

Pork and Deer Sausage

1¾ lb. ground deer meat
1¾ lb. ground pork (be sure it's
   fat)
1 tbsp. salt
1 tsp. cayenne pepper
⅛ tsp. garlic powder

1 tsp. cumin
1 tsp. poultry seasoning
⅛ tsp. sage
⅛ tsp. curry powder
1 tsp. dried mint

Mix all of the ingredients well, and shape into patties. Be sure you don't mix more than 3½ pounds at a time with this particular recipe. *Serves 6-8.*

Note: It's a good idea to grind the pork and venison together. Grind twice.

I believe Walter jus' tol Alma Picou dat the best sauce piquante he made was out of nutria rat, muskrat, an' coon all mixed together. But I don' exactly believe dat, no! I don' believe I don' believe dat, too, also. (Photo by David King Gleason)

VENISON SAUCE PIQUANTE

4 lb. round of venison, cut into 2-inch cubes
Salt, black pepper, and cayenne pepper
¾ cup bacon drippings
1 cup olive oil
1 cup all-purpose flour
2 8-oz. cans tomato sauce
8 medium-sized onions, chopped
2 bunches green onions, chopped
1 large bell pepper, chopped
1 cup celery, chopped
6 cups water
2 cloves garlic, chopped
2 tbsp. Worcestershire sauce
Juice from 2 lemons

Wash venison, season with salt and peppers, and fry in bacon drippings until brown. Remove from fat, and set aside.

Using olive oil and flour, make a roux with tomato sauce (see my roux recipe).

Add all the chopped seasonings, except garlic, cover, and simmer on low heat for about 1 hour.

Add venison to roux and chopped-seasonings mixture. Simmer for 30 minutes, covered. Add water, garlic, Worcestershire sauce, and lemon juice; cover; and let cook slowly for about 2 hours.

Serve over rice or spaghetti. *Serves 8-10.*

Note: For turtle sauce piquante, merely substitute 5 pounds of boned, washed turtle meat for venison. Lots of us Cajuns like turtle sauce piquante best.

I'm trimmin' the fat from dem venison roast dare 'cause fat on venison don' taste good, no. An' you can look at Sara an' see she's kinda nervous about the way I'm do dis. But we got it did, jus' the same. (Photo by David King Gleason)

VENISON ROAST

1 6- to 8-lb. venison roast
Vinegar
Water
Salt
Ground cayenne pepper
Olive oil
2 cups chopped onion

2 cloves chopped garlic
2 cups claret wine or dry red
   wine
2 cups water
1 small bay leaf
2 tbsp. Worcestershire sauce

Marinate venison in an equal mixture of vinegar and water for about 2 hours. Remove, and rinse well. Dry meat off. Rub salt and cayenne pepper into meat.

Preheat the oven to 300 or 350 degrees.

Cover bottom of baking pan with olive oil.

Place roast in pan and sear the meat on top of stove.

Add onions and garlic, then the wine and water. Add the bay leaf and Worcestershire sauce.

Place pan, covered, in the preheated oven. Cook until done; baste frequently. *Serves 8.*

Johnny Guitreau, he don' smoke some at all. 'Course, he eat about a dozen of them stogies ever' day, but that don' count none. (Photo by Bill Cooksey)

COOKING IN A BAG

There are several things you should remember when cooking in a bag. Follow these safety factors, an' you will have no problems, I garontee.

1. Check the bag to see if there are any holes in the bottom (of the bag, that's right). If so, don't use.

2. Always put 1 tablespoon of flour (at least) in the bag, and shake it up real good before you add anything else.

3. Punch holes in the top of the bag with a two-tine kitchen fork. Punch about 12 holes each time.

4. Never cook in an oven over 350 degrees.

Also, too, cooking in a bag is a great energy saver. Your meat cooks in about $\frac{1}{3}$ less time than usual and stays more moist in the bag.

BACKBONE PORK AND MUSHROOMS

8 backbones (each cut 1-inch
    thick)
Salt
Cayenne pepper
1 14-by-20-inch clear baking
    bag
2 tbsp. all-purpose flour
2 tbsp. dry parsley flakes

2 tsp. garlic powder
2 cups chopped onion
1 lb. fresh mushrooms
1 tbsp. Worcestershire sauce
¼ tsp. bitters (Peychaud or
    Angostura)
2 cups Sauterne wine or dry
    white wine

Preheat the oven to 325 degrees.

Season the meat with salt and pepper.

Shake the flour in the baking bag.

Place the meat in the bag, with a sprinkle of parsley and garlic powder. Add the onions and mushrooms. Stir Worcestershire sauce and bitters into the wine, and pour over the meat.

Close and tie the bag, and punch 12 holes in it with a two-tine kitchen fork.

Bake in the preheated oven until brown. *Serves 6-8.*

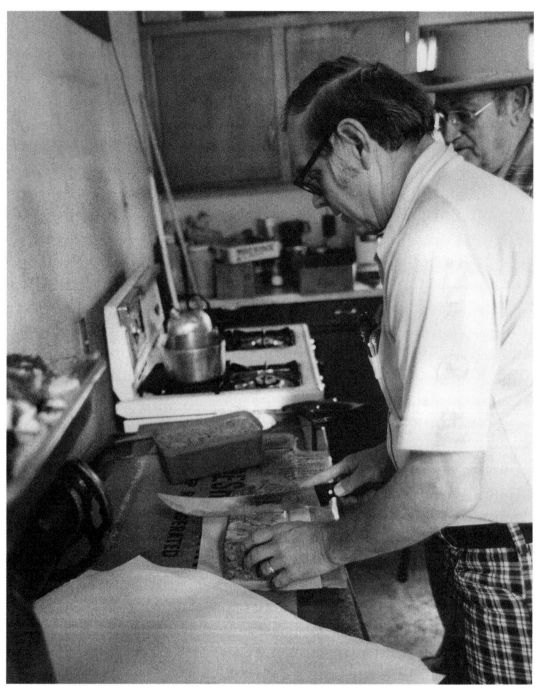

Murphy Brown, he put the insist on me dat I should try some of dis hogshead cheese what he's slicin' up. An' dat was a mistake wit' him. I done ate the whole damn t'ing! (Photo by David King Gleason)

Pork Roast

1 5-lb. pork roast (at least 5 lb.)
Peppers
Shallots
Garlic cloves
Salt
Ground cayenne pepper

1 large cooking bag
2 tbsp. flour
1 cup chopped green onions
1 cup wine
2 cups water

Preheat the oven to 325 degrees.

With a sharp knife, cut holes in various places on the roast, and stuff with peppers, shallots, and garlic on both sides. Salt and pepper both sides of the roast.

Grease baking pan.

Shake flour in the cooking bag, coating sides well.

In the bag, place the stuffed roast, chopped green onions, wine, and the water. Close and tie the bag, and punch 9 times in top of bag with a two-tine kitchen fork.

Put the whole mess in the pan, and bake for 3 hours. *Serves 8-10.*

Sittin' rat in front of dat beautiful roast what I got dare are two of the reasons why twin beds were invented. Dem are onions. An' what I'm sayin' here is you took ma onion away from me an' I couldn't cook not'ing hardly none at all any. (Photo by David King Gleason)

BONED RUMP ROAST IN A BAG

1 10-lb. roast beef, tied
5 cloves garlic
5 green onions (shallots)
5 hot pickled peppers
4 lb. mushrooms
Salt
Ground cayenne pepper
1 large cooking bag
1 tbsp. flour
8 large carrots
8 medium Irish potatoes

½ cup chopped parsley
1 cup chopped green onions
1 tsp. celery seed
2 tbsp. olive oil
2 cups Sauterne wine or dry
    white wine
1 cup water
2 tbsp. soy sauce
½ tsp. bitters (Peychaud or
    Angostura)

Preheat the oven to 350 degrees.

Punch 5 deep holes in the roast.

Stuff a garlic clove, shallot, and pepper into each hole in the roast.

Clean the mushrooms well.

Salt and pepper the roast.

Shake flour in the cooking bag and coat all sides well.

Place the roast in the cooking bag. Sprinkle a little salt on the mushrooms, carrots, and potatoes, and arrange them around the roast.

Add parsley, chopped green onions, celery seed, and olive oil. Pour in the wine, water, soy sauce, and bitters.

Tie the bag, and punch 9 times with a two-tine kitchen fork.

Bake in the preheated oven for 1½ hours. *Serves 10-12.*

Beef Shanks in a Bag

1 large turkey-size cooking
   bag
2 tbsp. flour
Salt
Ground cayenne pepper
6 shank bones, cut 2½ to 3
   inches thick
12 whole medium carrots
2 lb. potatoes, cut in half

6 small onions, cut in half
4 whole cloves garlic
1 can Ro-Tel tomatoes
1 tbsp. soy sauce
2 tbsp. Worcestershire sauce
½ tsp. bitters (Peychaud or
   Angostura)
2 cups Sauterne wine or dry
   white wine

Beef shanks are the cheapest cut of meat you can buy, and also the most tasty, because they are next to the bone.

Preheat the oven to 325 degrees.

Grease the baking pan.

Shake the flour in a turkey bag and coat sides well. Place the bag in the pan.

Salt and pepper the shanks. Put shanks in the bag, and place the vegetables over and around them evenly.

Combine Ro-Tel tomatoes, soy sauce, Worcestershire sauce, bitters, and wine. Mix well, and pour over the shanks and vegetables.

Tie the bag, and punch 12 holes in the top with a two-tine kitchen fork.

Bake in the preheated oven for 2 hours. *Serves 6-8.*

Beef Ribs in a Bag

4-6 ribs (each 4 inches long)
Salt
Cayenne pepper
Seasoned salt
1 large cooking bag
1 tbsp. flour

1 cup Sauterne wine or dry
  white wine
1 cup water
2 tbsp. Worcestershire sauce
1 tsp. garlic powder
2 tsp. onion powder

Preheat the oven to 325 degrees.

Season the ribs with salt, cayenne pepper, and seasoned salt.

Shake flour in a large plastic cooking bag, and coat sides thoroughly.

Place ribs in the baking bag.

Mix wine, water, Worcestershire sauce, garlic powder, and onion powder in a mixing bowl until the powders are dissolved. Pour into the bag around the ribs.

Tie the bag, and punch top of bag 12 times with a two-tine kitchen fork.

Bake in the preheated oven for 1 hour. *Serves 4.*

Jus' look at them beautifuls! An' we done brought them up on our own place, right there in Denham Springs, too! (Photo by Bill Cooksey)

Pot Roast Magnifique

1 large cooking bag
2 tbsp. flour
1 8-lb. chuck roast
Salt
Cayenne pepper
6 whole cloves garlic
6 pickled hot peppers
6 whole shallots

8 whole potatoes
8 whole carrots
4 whole onions
1 lb. fresh mushrooms
2 tbsp. Worcestershire sauce
2 cups wine
¼ tsp. bitters (Peychaud or
   Angostura)

Preheat the oven to 350 degrees.

Grease the baking pan.

Shake flour in a large cooking bag, and coat sides evenly.

Salt and pepper the roast.

Cut 6 holes in the roast, and stuff each hole with a garlic clove, a hot pepper, and a shallot. (Cut off the portion of the pepper and shallot sticking out of the hole.)

Place the stuffed chuck roast in the cooking bag, and then put it in the pan. Add to the bag, placing around the roast evenly, potatoes, carrots, onions, and mushrooms.

Mix the Worcestershire sauce, wine, and bitters. Pour over the ingredients in the bag, and tie.

Punch 12 holes in the top of the bag with a two-tine fork.

Bake in the preheated oven for about 2 or 3 hours. *Serves 6-10.*

"Ooh boy! Magnifique mean magnificent. An' dat's exactly how it taste, marvelmous, I garontee!"

MEAT LOAF

3 lb. ground round
1 tbsp. ground celery seed
1 tsp. garlic powder
1 tsp. dried mint
1 tsp. seasoned salt
1 tsp. salt
1 tbsp. parsley flakes
2 cups chopped onion
1 cup chopped green onions
1 cup chopped bell pepper
4 eggs, beaten well

1 tbsp. Worcestershire sauce
¼ tsp. bitters (Peychaud
   or Angostura)
1 tsp. Louisiana hot sauce
For red sauce: 2 cans (16 oz.
   each) tomato sauce
For brown sauce: 4 cans (8 oz.
   each) mushroom sauce
1 tbsp. flour
1 large cooking bag

Preheat the oven to 325 degrees.

Get you the biggest bowl you can find in your house, and mix all your ingredients together except the eggs, Worcestershire sauce, bitters, and Louisiana hot sauce.

In a separate bowl, mix the eggs, Worcestershire sauce, bitters, and hot sauce and beat really well. Mix everything together, and shape into a meat loaf.

Some people like a red sauce over meat loaf and some like brown. Pour preferred type of sauce over the meat loaf. If necessary, add a little water and a little wine (in equal amounts).

Shake flour in a cooking bag, and coat sides really well. Put the whole damn thing in the bag, and tie. The meat loaf will cook in about a third less time in the bag than usual. (Don't forget to punch holes in the cooking bag with a two-tine kitchen fork!)

Bake in the preheated oven for about 1 hour (or until brown). *Serves 8-10.*

"Let me tol' you somet'ing about dat meat loaf. It's one of dem Cajun dish what taste even better the nex' day on sammiches. It soak up all dem seasoning, an' it's good. (Dat depend if dey any lef', which I doubt.)"

CHICKEN I DON'T KNOW

1 turkey-size cooking bag
2 tbsp. flour
2 big fryers, quartered
Salt
Ground cayenne pepper
4 cups onion, chopped
1 cup celery, chopped
1 cup bell pepper, chopped
1 cup parsley, chopped
1 tbsp. garlic, chopped
1 small bay leaf
1½ cups Sauterne wine or dry
   white wine
1 tbsp. soy sauce
1 tbsp. Worcestershire sauce
½ tsp. bitters (Peychaud
   or Angostura)
1 cup water

Grease the baking pan. Preheat the oven to 350 degrees.

Shake flour in the bag, and coat sides well. Put the bag in the pan.

Salt and pepper the fryers, and place them in bag.

Add the onion, celery, bell pepper, parsley, garlic, and bay leaf.

Combine the wine, soy sauce, Worcestershire sauce, and bitters. Pour over the ingredients in the cooking bag. Pour 1 cup water over the ingredients in the cooking bag, and tie.

Punch 12 holes in the top of the bag with a cooking fork.

Bake in the preheated oven for 1½ hours or until the chicken comes off the bone. *Serves 6-10.*

"Chicken I Don't Know. I mus' tol' you about dis. I didn't know what the hell to call it! But I know one t'ing about it. It sure taste good, I garontee!"

TURKEY IN A BAG

1 turkey	1 tbsp. flour
Salt and pepper	1 turkey-sized cooking bag
Cooking oil	

Preheat the oven to 325 degrees.

Clean the turkey well, both inside and out. Sprinkle with salt and pepper. Grease the turkey all over with cooking oil.

Shake flour in a large cooking bag, and coat sides well.

Put the turkey in the bag, tie, and punch 9 holes with a kitchen fork.

Bake in the preheated oven until the turkey browns. *Serves 6-10.*

Note: You can put potatoes around the turkey if you want. Actually, you can put anything next to it, and it will taste good! Also, too, you can put dressing in the turkey. But don't you forget to sew it up.

QUAIL IN A BAG

1 tbsp. flour	1 lb. fresh mushrooms
1 large cooking bag	Bay leaf
6 quail	1 cup Sauterne wine or dry
Salt	white wine
Ground cayenne pepper	½ lemon
1 cup chopped onion	1 cup water
½ cup chopped bell pepper	

Grease baking pan. Preheat the oven to 350 degrees.

Shake flour in a large cooking bag, and coat sides evenly.

Split dressed birds down the back. Salt and pepper them, and rub seasonings well into the birds.

Put the birds in the bag. Add all the other ingredients to the bag, and tie.

Punch 12 holes in the top of the bag with a two-tine kitchen fork.

Bake in the preheated oven for 45 minutes. *Serves 4-6.*

WILD GOOSE IN A BAG

1 or 2 large geese
1 turkey-sized cooking bag
1 tbsp. flour
Salt and cayenne pepper to
   taste
6 large onions
1 pkg. large, fresh mushrooms
10 small potatoes
3 cups Sauterne wine or dry
   white wine

2 tbsp. Worcestershire sauce
1 tbsp. soy sauce
2 cloves garlic
1 tsp. celery salt
1 cup water
¼ tsp. bitters (Peychaud
   or Angostura)

Preheat the oven to 325 or 350 degrees.

Shake flour in the cooking bag, and coat all sides well. Rub salt and cayenne pepper well into the birds.

Put the goose (or geese) in the bag, and surround it with onions, mushrooms, and potatoes.

Mix together the wine, Worcestershire sauce, soy sauce, garlic, celery salt, water, and bitters. Pour the sauce over the goose.

Put everything in the bag, and tie it up. Punch 12 holes in the bag with a two-tine kitchen fork.

Bake in the preheated oven until you look in there and see that it's done.

Cook some rice on the side to serve with it. *Serves 6-8.*

"I got to tol' you somet'ing. I was trainin' a man to be a safety engineer down in South Louisiana. He look at me one day and say, 'Justin, you know what a wild goose is?' I say, 'What.' He say, 'About dat far off center!' I started to kill 'em!"

*You can look at me an' tol', when I shop on dem grocery store, I should
never go dare hungry like I am here, no.* (Photo by David King Gleason)

EGG DISHES

Sunny-Side Up

I was in Oklahoma City a number of years ago, back when the old Biltmore Hotel was still there. I was training a man to be a safety engineer for Falcon-Seaboard Drilling Company out of Tulsa. Glen Lewis was his name, and he was funny as hell!

The Biltmore Hotel had the most beautiful collection of Indian paintings and art I ever saw. We were walking along the street near the hotel. It was 114 degrees, and that was in the days before heat indexes!

Glen said, "You know, Justin, it's hot enough to fry an egg on that sidewalk."

So I said, "Glen, go get a couple of eggs, and let's see."

I cracked those two eggs on that sidewalk, sunny-side up, of course, and they fried just as pretty as any eggs I ever saw.

This is true, now. A policeman walked up. "Hey, what the hell are y'all doing?" he asked us.

I said, "What the hell it look like? I'm fryin' eggs. Can't you see that?"

He could not believe that, and he just turned and walked away. I think he thought we were crazy!

BAKED EGGS

Olive oil
Eggs
Muffin tin

Benedictine, Cointreau, creme de menthe, or brandy

Preheat the oven to 325 degrees.

Put a drop or two of olive oil and one egg in each muffin tin cup.

To each egg, add a couple of drops of either Benedictine, Cointreau, creme de menthe, or brandy.

Bake in the preheated oven. Watch them, and take them out when they are as hard as you like them.

"I love eggs. I cooked them 39 different ways one day. Travis Lobell had an egg farm, and we decided to see how many different ways we could do it. We took muffin tins, and we put Cointreau in one, brandy in one, rice, all kinds of things. It's not hard to get 39 ways when you're a damn fool and have fun doing it, and especially when you've got a friend 'egging' you on!"

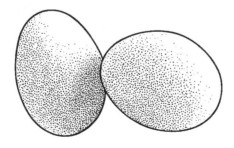

You see dat bottle I got on my hand? Dat is at least *fo' hundred an' forty-fo' yards of red-pepper hell, I garontee!* (Photo by David King Gleason)

Peppy Pickled Eggs

18-20 large eggs	2 tbsp. salt
1 bay leaf	1 tbsp. chili powder
6-8 hot peppers	Apple cider vinegar
4 cloves garlic, cut in half	Water

After boiling and peeling the eggs, puncture them several times with a toothpick.

Put the eggs into a one-gallon sterilized jar. Place bay leaf in the jar and layer the peppers and garlic with the eggs. Repeat the layers until all of the ingredients are used. Add salt and chili powder.

Fill jar with heated vinegar and water (equal amounts of each). (Don't boil the vinegar and water.) Cover the eggs and fill the jar completely. Seal the jar, invert, and shake well to mix the seasonings. *Pickles 18-20 eggs.*

Note: Wait a week before eating. These will keep at least 3 weeks in the refrigerator.

Rice Omelet (Egg Jambalaya)

3 eggs, beaten well	½ cup chopped green onion
½ cup cooked rice	Bacon drippings

Mix together the beaten eggs, rice, and chopped onion.

Heat bacon drippings in an omelet pan.

When drippings are hot, pour in the egg mixture, and cook until the eggs are done. *Serves 4.*

FIRM OMELET

4 eggs   ⅛ tsp. paprika
4 tbsp. water   1½ tbsp. butter
½ tsp. salt

Beat the eggs until well blended. Add water, salt, and paprika.

Melt the butter in a skillet. When this is fairly hot, add the egg mixture, and cook over low heat. (It is best to cook it in an omelet pan over a medium fire.)

Lift the edges of the omelet with a pancake turner, and tilt the skillet to permit the uncooked custard to run to the bottom. When it is all an even consistency, increase the heat to brown the bottom slightly. Fold over the omelet and serve. *Serves 4-6.*

"If you don' got no omelet pan, dat's bad. It take practice to fold over dem egg an' make dat omelet purty an' nice. You put dem egg dare in a plain ol' pan an' it's gonna run all over hell an' back."

ANCHOVY OMELET

4 eggs   1 tsp. chopped parsley
1 clove garlic   ¾ tsp. anchovy paste

Beat the eggs.

Rub a small bowl with garlic. Put the eggs in the bowl, and stir in the parsley and anchovy paste.

Cook in a greased pan over medium fire until firm. *Serves 4-6.*

OMELET AND SAUSAGES

6 breakfast sausages   **Parsley for garnish**
4 eggs   **Tomato sauce**

Broil 6 breakfast sausages, and drain them on absorbent paper. Keep them hot.

Beat the eggs, pour them into omelet pan, and cook over medium heat.

Place the sausages in the center of the omelet, and fold it over. Garnish with parsley and serve with tomato sauce. *Serves 4-6.*

CHEESE OMELET

4 eggs   **2 tbsp. chopped green pepper**
½ cup grated cheese   **(if desired)**
2 tbsp. chopped parsley

Preheat the oven to 275 degrees.

Beat the eggs.

Sprinkle with cheese, parsley, and green pepper, and put into a small casserole dish.

Bake the omelet in a preheated, slow oven until the cheese is melted. Serve with a parsley garnish. *Serves 4-6.*

Omelet with Creole Sauce and Peas

4 eggs
2 cups condensed tomato soup
2 tbsp. butter or margarine
2 cups cooked English peas
½ cup green pepper, chopped

½ cup onion, chopped
½ cup celery, chopped
½ cup olives, chopped
½ cup dill pickles, chopped

Beat the 4 eggs, and cook the eggs in an omelet pan over medium heat.

Mix together the rest of the ingredients, heat thoroughly, and pour the sauce around the cooked omelet. Serve with a parsley garnish. *Serves 4-6.*

Lobster or Crabmeat Omelet

4 eggs
1 tbsp. minced onion
2 tbsp. butter or bacon
    drippings

1 tbsp. chopped celery
    (or more, if desired)
¾ cup diced lobster
    or crabmeat

Beat the eggs, and cook in an omelet pan over medium heat.
Sauté the onion in the butter.
Add celery and lobster or crabmeat, and simmer for 3 minutes.
Before folding the omelet, spread it with the mixture. Fold and serve garnished with parsley. *Serves 4-6.*

"I like eggs mos' anyway, 'cept raw. Dese are 'good eggs,' I garontee!"

QUICHE LORRAINE

4 eggs, slightly beaten
2 cups grated cheddar or Swiss cheese
½ cup chopped onion
2 tbsp. chopped pimiento
2 tbsp. chopped bell pepper
2 unbaked pie shells
8 strips bacon, crumbled

Paprika
1½ cups half & half (or an equal mixture of milk and cream)
1 cup chopped ham
Salt
Pepper
2 tbsp. flour

Preheat the oven to 400 degrees.

Blend all of the ingredients together, and pour into unbaked pie shells.

Bake in the preheated oven for 15-20 minutes or until firm and stiff. *Serves 4-6.*

The law don' got me, I got him. An' we been talkin' about cookin', an' he's a damn good cook. His name is C.J. ("J.J.") Berthelot. (C.J. is his fron' name.) An' like I tol' you, he's a damn good cook, I garontee! (Photo by David King Gleason)

VEGETABLES AND MORE

Crowley Rice Festival

I was a young man when I helped create the annual Rice Festival in Crowley back in 1936. Nobody thought I was old enough to handle such a big project.

Bob Schlicher, manager of Louisiana State Rice Mill in Crowley, was cochairman with me.

I looked in the *Farmer's Almanac* to see which month we'd be least likely to get rained on, and it was October. So that's when we held the Rice Festival.

As to why we decided to have the festival, that's simple: farmers couldn't get rid of the rice, so we had to promote it. The federal government had a parity on rice. I think it was $1.65 a barrel. They couldn't get less than that, but they couldn't sell it.

One of the things we did, we decided to have a mass wedding and spray the couples with rice from an airplane. The priest said, "You can't have this wedding; it's a travesty of the sacred state of matrimony."

We started out with 50 couples, but because of the priest's objections, all but four couples withdrew. We sprayed them with rice from an airplane anyway and gave each couple a hundred pounds of rice.

We were determined to sell rice, and we did. We made the newspapers in 43 of the 48 states.

Governor Dick Leche's public relations man, George Dye, had all kinds of promotional ideas. We even had girls dressed up like rice stalks. They were very pretty girls!

Rice (Long Grain)

Place as much rice as you need in a heavy pan. Cover with water until the water is first-joint deep above the level of the rice. Use the middle finger to measure, since the first joint of the middle finger is the same length in every normal-sized adult, believe it or not!

Add salt to taste, usually about 2 teaspoonfuls. Place over hottest flame, and let it come to rapid boil. Boil in this fashion until you can't see any water bubbling in the holes that will appear in the surface.

Then, turn heat to simmer, and simmer for 30-40 minutes, with pan lid on. Don't even peek at it until you're ready to serve it. Above all, don't panic. If you follow this carefully, you won't burn a damn t'ing, I garontee!

Dirty Rice

2 cups water
2 lb. lean ground beef
2 lb. lean ground pork
1 lb. chicken giblets, ground
1 cup yellow onions, diced
1 cup diced shallots (green onions)
½ cup diced bell peppers
¼ cup garlic (preferably ground)
¼ cup parsley, finely chopped
2 cups celery, finely chopped
4 bay leaves
1 tsp. black pepper
3 tbsp. Worcestershire sauce
½ lb. margarine or butter
Salt
2 cans cream of mushroom soup

With about 2 cups of water, mix all meats together in a heavy pot, on a medium-hot burner. Add all the above seasoning ingredients except the cream of mushroom soup at the start of cooking.

Cook on medium heat approximately 4 hours, stirring often.

Add the cream of mushroom soup, and continue cooking for 30 minutes.

Boil 2 pounds long-grain rice (see my recipe). Let rice cook completely.

After rice has cooked, mix thoroughly with the meat ingredients.

Allow to steam or cook on a low heat for approximately 30 minutes before serving. *Serves 10.*

ASPARAGUS WITH SHRIMP CASSEROLE

2 tbsp. olive oil
1 can green asparagus
1½ cups American cheese,
    grated
½ cup Romano cheese, grated
2 cups boiled, peeled shrimp
2 eggs
1 cup Sauterne wine or dry
    white wine

2 tsp. Worcestershire sauce
1 tsp. Louisiana hot sauce
1½ tsp. salt
1 can cream of mushroom
    soup
¾ cup bread crumbs

Preheat the oven to 350 degrees.

Put olive oil in bottom of casserole, and spread asparagus over it.

Then add a layer of American and Romano cheese, followed by a layer of shrimp, and topped by another layer of the cheeses. Continue this process of alternating layers of shrimp and cheese until casserole is ¾ full with a cheese layer on top.

In a bowl, beat the two eggs, and gradually add, as you beat, 1 cup of wine. Continue to beat until the mixture smells like eggnog. Add Worcestershire, hot sauce, and salt; and pour over ingredients in casserole.

Pour cream of mushroom soup over the casserole, and top with bread crumbs.

Bake in the preheated oven for one hour. *Serves 6.*

"Company drop' in on us one Sunday an', natcherly, we got to cook for them somet'ing. This here casserole was what come out of the kitchen, after I got through foolin' aroun' out there awhile.

"It turn' out so good, now it's a favorite at our house. In fac', it so good I believe you can t'row in you' ol' rubber boot an' not hurt it none, too."

ASPARAGUS-TUNA CASSEROLE

2 tbsp. olive oil
2 cups onion, chopped
2 14½-oz. cans asparagus,
   drained into a cup
3 cups grated cheddar cheese
1 cup fresh, parboiled
   mushrooms
Lemon-pepper seasoning
1 large can (12½ oz.) tuna,
   drained and broken up

Parmesan cheese
2 eggs
½ cup Sauterne or dry white
   wine
½ cup asparagus juice
1 tsp. salt
1 cup seasoned bread crumbs

Preheat the oven to 350 degrees.

Sauté the onions in olive oil.

Arrange in a casserole dish, one layer for each: the asparagus, cheese, and mushrooms.

Sprinkle with lemon-pepper seasoning.

Mix tuna with the sautéed onion. Layer this, along with another layer of cheese, and sprinkle Parmesan and lemon-pepper seasoning on the top.

Beat eggs, wine, and asparagus juice. Add salt. Pour over all. Sprinkle bread crumbs on top.

Bake in the preheated oven until bread crumbs are brown. *Serves 4-6.*

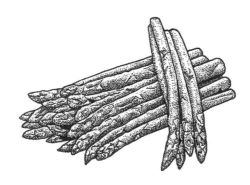

DRIED RED BEANS

1 lb. dried red kidney beans	Claret wine or dry red wine
2 large onions, chopped	Water
2 cloves garlic, chopped	Olive oil
1 green hot pepper, chopped, or 1½ tsp. Louisiana hot sauce	¼ lb. ham, salt shoulder, or pickled shoulder of pork
	Salt

Wash beans well, getting all the grit and rocks out of them. Place in an earthenware or glass bowl.

Add chopped onions, garlic, and hot pepper to the beans. If you don't have a hot pepper, add Louisiana hot sauce. Pour an equal mixture of wine and water over the beans so that they are covered by an inch or more of liquid.

Let these beans soak, or marinate, overnight. You may have to add 1 cup wine and 1 cup water to them before you go to bed or before you put them on in the morning.

The next morning, cover the bottom of a heavy pot (preferably cast iron) with about ½ cup olive oil. Add whichever meat that you have decided to use, and heat.

Pour beans and the mixture in which they have marinated into pot. Add water if necessary.

Bring to a good boil, then turn fire down and cook slowly for several hours until done. Add salt just before you think the beans are done, and let it cook into the beans.

Serve these beans over steamed rice. *Serves 4-6.*

Note: This recipe may be applied to white beans or dried peas, using Sauterne or dry white wine in place of claret.

"Sometimes, when I'm real hongry—which is mos' of the time—I puts a slice of boiled ham on top of them red beans an' rice. Hoo, boy! That's plumb good!"

Red Beans with Rice and Smoked Sausage

1 lb. dried red kidney beans	Olive oil
2 large onions	2 lb. smoked sausage
2 cloves garlic	¼ lb. ham, salt shoulder, or
1 green hot pepper or ½ tsp.	pickled pork shoulder
Louisiana hot sauce	Salt
Claret wine	Steamed rice
Water	

Wash beans well, getting all grit and rocks out. Place in earthen-ware or glass bowl.

Chop up onions, garlic, and pepper and add to the beans. Add pepper or Louisiana hot sauce.

Pour an equal mixture of wine and water over beans so they are well covered by an inch or more of liquid.

Let the beans soak, or marinate, overnight. You may have to add 1 cup wine and 1 cup water to them by bedtime or before you cook them in the morning.

The next morning, cover the bottom of a heavy pot with about ½ cup olive oil.

Add sausage and meat, and heat. Pour the beans and marinade mixture into the pot, along with some water, if necessary.

Bring to a good boil, turn fire down, and cook slowly for several hours until done. Add salt just before beans are done, and let it cook into them.

Serve over steamed rice. *Serves 4-6.*

Variation: This recipe may also be applied to white or pinto beans, or dried peas, using dry white wine in place of claret.

"When I was coming up, red beans were eaten 'most any day we had them. They were not served only on Monday, which was wash day, as so many people believe. They were good any day of the week!"

This is a little snack we done cook up one night at the Houston Press Club. Wasn' but twenty-two differen' dishes on the menu. (Photo by Bill Cooksey)

RED BEANS AND RICE AU VIN

2 lb. dried red beans, washed
    thoroughly and drained
2 medium onions, chopped
1 small clove garlic, chopped
2 to 3 cups Sauterne wine or
    dry white wine
1 tbsp. Worcestershire sauce

1 to 2 tsp. Louisiana hot sauce
Water
½ cup olive oil
2 slices thick bacon, cubed
Salt to taste
Cooked rice

Place beans in an earthenware or glass bowl, and add onions, garlic, wine, Worcestershire sauce, and Louisiana hot sauce. Add enough water to cover beans by about an inch. Marinate overnight.

The next day, pour olive oil into a pot big enough to hold all of the beans with ease.

Fry the bacon in olive oil until soft, but not brown.

Add bean mixture and more water as needed. Cook on medium heat until tender.

After the beans are tender, salt to taste, and cook until done to your taste.

Serve over rice. *Serves 8.*

BARBECUED BEANS

¾ lb. ground beef
½ lb. hot sausage (patties)
8 to 10 slices crisp bacon
4 16-oz. cans pork and beans
1 tsp. cayenne pepper
¾ cup molasses or honey
¾ cup barbecue sauce
1 tbsp. Worcestershire sauce
½ tsp. salt

Couple good dashes of
    Louisiana hot sauce
1½ cups finely chopped onion
½ tsp. bitters (Peychaud
    or Angostura)
1 tsp. dried mint
1 tsp. Liquid Smoke
Steamed rice

Preheat the oven to 350 degrees.

Cook ground beef and sausage until well done. Break meats up into a fine texture with a fork while cooking. Drain off the fat.

Cook bacon crisp, and crush over the other meats just cooked.

Open bean cans, and drain off what juice you can.

Mix the meats and all other ingredients with the beans.

Bake in a Pyrex or other oven-casserole dish in the preheated oven for 45 minutes. Serve hot. *Serves 4-8.*

"Each time this stuff is reheated, it seems to taste better. It also freezes very well for later use. This stuff is plenty good, I garontee!"

BLACK-EYED PEAS

1 lb. dried black-eyed peas
2 large onions, chopped
2 cloves garlic, chopped
1 green hot pepper, chopped,
 or 1½ tsp. Louisiana hot
 sauce
Sauterne wine or dry white
 wine

Water
½ cup olive oil
¼ pound ham, salt shoulder,
 or pickled pork shoulder
Salt
Steamed rice

Wash peas well, getting all the grit and rocks out of them. Place in an earthenware or glass bowl. Add chopped onion, garlic, and pepper or hot sauce to the peas. Pour an equal mixture of wine and water over the peas so they are covered by an inch or more of liquid. Let soak overnight. You may have to add 1 cup wine and 1 cup water to them before you go to bed or before you put them on in the morning.

The next morning, cover the bottom of a heavy pot (preferably cast iron) with about ½ cup olive oil. Add the meat you have decided to use and heat. Pour peas and the mixture in which they have marinated into the pot. (Add water if necessary.)

Bring to a good boil, then turn the fire down, and cook slowly for several hours until done. Add salt just before the peas are done. Cook a few minutes longer, so the salt will be absorbed.

Serve over steamed rice. *Serves 4-8.*

BLACK-EYED PEA JAMBALAYA

2 qt. water
½ lb. bacon, cut into 1-inch
  cubes
2 cups black-eyed peas (fresh,
  frozen, or dried)

1 tsp. salt
1 cup uncooked long-grain rice
Sliced bacon

Cook the bacon in 2 quarts of water for about 1 hour, then add the black-eyed peas. Continue cooking for 30 minutes, or until the peas are almost tender.

Add salt and rice, and boil about 15 to 18 minutes longer.

Drain the peas and rice thoroughly, and place in a casserole dish in a warm oven for a few minutes until rice is fluffy.

Serve with sliced bacon on the top. *Serves 4-6.*

BLACK-EYED PEA BALLS

3 cups cooked black-eyed
  peas, drained
1 cup ground beef
½ cup finely chopped green
  onions
Salt
Ground cayenne pepper to
  taste

2 eggs, well beaten
1 tbsp. Worcestershire sauce
Seasoned bread crumbs
All-purpose flour
Cooking oil

Mix drained peas, meat, and chopped onions well. Salt and pepper to taste.

Beat the eggs and Worcestershire sauce together thoroughly, and blend into the peas and meat. Add bread crumbs until the mixture is cohesive enough to roll in flour. Shape into balls.

Cook in oil heated to 325 degrees. Balls will float when done. *Serves 4-10.*

Field or Crowder Peas

2 or 3 lb. fresh peas	1 large onion
Olive oil	1 small clove garlic
¼ lb. lean salt or pickled pork	Fresh green hot pepper
3 cups Sauterne wine or dry	or 1 tsp. Louisiana hot sauce
white wine	Salt

Shell and wash peas, and place in colander to drain.

Cover bottom of pot with olive oil. Cube salt meat, and fry in olive oil for about 5 minutes. Add peas, then wine.

Dice onion and garlic, and put into the pot.

Add pepper or hot sauce. Add water if any liquid is needed.

Cook until peas are tender and done. Salt to taste after peas have become tender. *Serves 8.*

Variations: This recipe can be used for fresh butter or lima beans. Frozen beans or peas may be used; *jus' don' shell an' wash 'em.*

"Now that the sout' done rising again, you can get field or crowder peas in mos' any grocery store in the U.S. an' A. But when you fixin' these, be sure an don' salt them until they is done. Saltin' them befo' they done make them tough as ol' mule hide."

Snap or String Beans au Vin

2 lb. fresh snap beans	2 or 3 cups Sauterne wine or
½ cup olive oil	dry white wine
2 slices thick bacon, cubed	1 tbsp. Worcestershire sauce
2 medium-sized onions,	Louisiana Hot Sauce (cayenne)
chopped	Salt
1 small clove garlic, chopped	Water if needed

Snap and string the beans.

Pour olive oil into a pot big enough to hold all the beans with ease (preferably a cast-iron pot).

Put bacon in olive oil, and fry until soft, not brown.

Add beans, onions, garlic, and wine. Add Worcestershire sauce, and season with Louisiana hot sauce to taste, approximately 1 to 2 teaspoons should do.

After beans have become tender, salt to taste, and cook until done to your taste. *Serves 8.*

"If you can't get them fresh beans, bought you'self some froze one.

"But when you cook them, jus' throw away them instructs on the outside package.

"What you do with them is toss them in the pot wit' all them other ingredients, like the recipe done tol' you, and cook them until they are tender. Then you salt them to you' taste."

Bienville's Vegetable Garden

Soon after New Orleans was founded, French Governor Bienville obtained royal grants to lands just north of the colony. But in 1719, the king forbade governors to own plantations, although he did allow them to have "vegetable gardens."

Governor Bienville quickly chose 53½ arpents (an arpent is a little more than an acre) of land right in the middle of what is now downtown New Orleans as his "vegetable garden." He also hired several German families to live on the land and farm it. Then he sold the rest of his 213 arpents to French settlers, in return for annual payments in money and produce.

What he did was legal, but it sure sounds like Louisiana politics!

Broccoli with Rice

½ cup bacon drippings
1 onion, finely chopped
1 celery rib, finely chopped
1 pkg. frozen chopped broccoli
1 can cream of chicken soup
1 large jar Cheese Whiz

1½ cups cooked rice
Salt
Cayenne pepper
Louisiana hot sauce
Seasoned bread crumbs

Preheat the oven to 325 degrees.

Sauté the onions and celery in bacon drippings.

Boil the broccoli, and drain; mix with soup and cheese. Add the onion and celery.

Stir in the rice, and season with salt, pepper, and hot sauce to taste. Sprinkle seasoned bread crumbs on top.

Bake in a greased casserole dish in the preheated oven for 45 minutes. *Serves 4-6.*

Brussels Sprouts au Gratin

Olive oil
Brussels sprouts, cooked and
  drained
1 onion, sliced
1 cup Romano or Parmesan
  cheese
1 cup grated Swiss cheese

1 cup grated American cheese
Salt
Cayenne pepper
1 cup Sauterne wine or dry
  white wine

Preheat the oven to 375 degrees.

Cover the bottom and the sides of a casserole dish with olive oil. Place in the casserole layers of brussels sprouts, sliced onion, and the three kinds of cheese. Salt and pepper to taste.

Repeat the layers until the casserole is full. Season each layer with salt and pepper. Pour wine over the whole mess.

Bake in the preheated oven for 1 hour or until tender.

CABBAGE ROLL À LA MARIE

1 lb. ground meat
1 cup raw rice
1 egg
1 onion, chopped
1 clove garlic, minced
Cayenne pepper to taste

¼ cup claret wine or dry red
  wine
1 head cabbage
1 8-oz. can tomato sauce
  or 1 cup ketchup
½ can (4 oz.) water

Mix the ground meat, rice, egg, onion, garlic, pepper, and wine together in a bowl.

Separate cabbage into leaves, trimming away all the tough part of the stem of each leaf. Place leaves in a pan of water to tenderize.

When soft, place a generous tablespoon of the meat-rice mixture into each cabbage leaf and roll edges of leaf around it. The roll may be secured by toothpick.

Put the rolls into a saucepan. Pour mixture of tomato sauce and water over the rolls.

Cook on low heat for 30 to 40 minutes. *Serves 4-6.*

"In my travels—an' I is a much-traveled Cajun, I garontee—I have done eat mos' every kind cookin' they is. But, to tol' the trut', I would rather eat at Marie O'Neill's house than jus' about any place I can thought of.

"An' I would jus' about rather eat this cabbage roll than anythin' I can thought of right at this moment, here.

"You ain' gonna believe cabbage an' meat roll together like this could taste so good as this do, but it do."

BOILED CABBAGE DINNER

Olive oil
1 medium-sized cabbage, quartered
4-6 large onions, peeled
4-6 medium Irish potatoes, peeled
4-6 carrots, peeled

3 cups Sauterne wine or dry white wine
3 cups water
Louisiana hot sauce
Salt
1½-2 lb. smoked pork sausage or cubed ham

Use a pot large enough to hold all of the vegetables and meat. Cover bottom of pot with olive oil, at least ¼ cup and maybe a little more.

Put cabbage into pot. Then add the whole onions, potatoes, and carrots.

Next add wine and water. After adding Louisiana hot sauce and salt to taste, bring to a boil.

Add meat. Add more water if necessary.

Cook until meat and potatoes are done. This can be eaten as a full meal. *Serves 4-6.*

"This is one of them dishes you can cook when you don' feel like cookin' much at all. When you don' feel like dirtyin' up a whole lot of pots, an' you don' feel like watchin' anything real close, cook this.

"Oh, yes, an' befo' I forgot to tol' you this, when I say cube the sausage or ham, I don' mean little bitty pieces, none either. I mean maybe 2-inch squares, so you' gonna feel like you' eatin' somethin'."

STUFFED CUCUMBERS

8 cucumbers, sliced lengthwise
2 tbsp. olive oil
1½ cups onion, chopped
½ cup celery, chopped
½ cup fresh mushroom stems
   (parboil until tender),
   chopped
1 heaping tbsp. dried parsley
1 large clove garlic, minced

½ cup Sauterne wine or dry
   white wine
1 cup canned shrimp, chopped
1 cup seasoned bread crumbs
1 tbsp. Worcestershire sauce
2 tsp. salt
2 tsp. Louisiana hot sauce
Romano cheese, grated

Preheat the oven to 350 degrees.

Cut the cucumbers in half, lengthwise, and parboil them in water until tender.

Scrape the insides out, and chop up in a bowl.

Sauté in olive oil the onion, celery, mushroom stems, and parsley; add garlic after a little juice is formed.

Pour ½ cup wine and ½ cup water in a baking dish.

Add the remaining ingredients except for the cheese and stir everything together.

Stuff each cucumber shell with the mixture, and sprinkle with Romano cheese.

Bake in the preheated oven until brown (less than 1 hour). *Serves 10-12.*

"Dis stuffed cucumbers, people laugh at me about dis. Dis dish was what come out of the kitchen after I got t'rough foolin' around dare for awhile.

"The secret is to use what you got. You could use anyt'ing an' it will turn out good. I believe you could t'row in a old shoe, an' it won't be bad, no! I garontee it will be the mos' bes' t'ing you ate ever."

EGGPLANT AND CHEESE

Eggplant, peeled and sliced
Salt
Cayenne pepper
Olive oil
Bacon drippings

Soy sauce
Swiss cheese, grated
Romano or Parmesan cheese,
  grated
American cheese, sliced

Salt and pepper the eggplant. Fry the sliced eggplant in a mixture of olive oil and bacon drippings. Drain well after frying.

Layer the eggplant in a heavy platter. Sprinkle soy sauce and Romano and Swiss cheeses on each layer except the top. Place a layer of sliced American cheese on the top. Heat in a warm oven until the cheese melts.

"This is good cold and chopped like chocolate candy. It can also be used as an appetizer. How many servings does this make? It depends on how much eggplant you've got and how much cheese you decide to use with it. This is delicious no matter how many people eat it!"

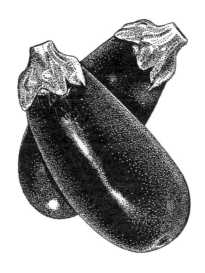

EGGPLANTS

3 medium eggplants
Salted water to soak eggplants
Olive oil
2 cups water
½ tsp. salt
1 cup white bread crumbs
1 cup Italian-style bread
   crumbs
½ cup Romano cheese, grated
4 eggs

½ cup Sauterne wine or dry
   white wine
4 small onions
2 cloves garlic
2 tsp. Louisiana hot sauce
1 tbsp. Worcestershire sauce
2 cups American cheese,
   grated
½ lb. Swiss cheese, sliced

Preheat the oven to 325 degrees.

Peel and chop eggplants, and soak about 30 minutes in salt water. Drain.

Put 2 tbsp. olive oil in bottom of pan with 2 cups water. Parboil eggplants until they can be mashed with a fork. Mash and beat. Add salt, two types of bread crumbs, and Romano cheese. Fold together.

Beat eggs in Sauterne wine. Puree onions and garlic. Mix these two ingredients with the well-beaten eggs, then add hot sauce and Worcestershire sauce. Add to eggplant mixture. Mix well.

Prepare large casserole with 3½ tablespoons olive oil in bottom. Put about a 1-inch layer of eggplant mixture in the casserole, then a thick layer of grated American cheese. Add another layer of eggplant, then another thick layer of American cheese.

Cover casserole with thin slices of Swiss cheese, and bake in the preheated oven until brown on top. *Serves 6-8.*

"You gonna make you'self some new frien's with this recipe, I garontee! When they axe you what is this wondermous aroma and this marvelmous taste, you can tell them it smell that way and taste that way because you use three different kinds of cheese, not jus' one. This is what really gives it a unusual flavor.

"Only maybe you don' want to told them you' secret some at all. In that case, jus' smile real sweetlike, an' tell them it ain' none of they dam' business how you did that."

Eggplant Casserole à la Justin

4 qt. chopped eggplant
Salted water to marinate
 eggplant
1 cup Sauterne wine or dry
 white wine
2 cups water
2 tbsp. Worcestershire sauce
2 tsp. Louisiana hot sauce
1 tbsp. soy sauce
2 tbsp. olive oil
2 cups chopped onion

1 cup chopped bell pepper
1 cup chopped parsley
1 tsp. onion powder
1 tsp. garlic powder
1 tsp. celery salt
1 tsp. butter-flavored salt
Salt
1 cup shrimp
1 cup tuna
2 eggs
Progresso bread crumbs

Preheat the oven to 350 degrees.

Marinate the eggplant in the salted water, rinse, and drain.

Cook eggplant in a mixture of wine, water, Worcestershire, hot sauce, and soy sauce until it can be mashed. Pour it into a colander, saving the juice.

Sauté the onions, bell pepper, and parsley in olive oil until clear or tender.

Add onion powder, garlic powder, celery salt, butter-flavored salt, and salt to taste.

Combine this mixture, the shrimp, and tuna with the eggplant. Mix well, using a little of the juice that was saved for extra flavor.

Beat the eggs and fold in.

Place in a buttered casserole dish, and top with bread crumbs.

Bake in the preheated oven 45 minutes to an hour. *Serves 8-12.*

You noted dat I'm overlook real good dare to see dat Murphy Brown cut dis pickled shoulder of pig jus' rat for me so's I can season some good mustard greens an' cabbage an' all kinds of vegetables like dat. (Photo by David King Gleason)

Mustard Greens au Vin

4 bunches fresh mustard greens	Salt
Olive oil	Fresh green hot pepper or
2 to 3 cups Sauterne wine or dry white wine	Louisiana hot sauce (cayenne)

Clean greens well by washing three times.

Cover bottom of pot (preferably a cast-iron pot) with about ⅛ inch of olive oil.

Place greens in pot, and pour wine over them. Put one whole pod of green hot pepper or 1 teaspoon of Louisiana hot sauce (cayenne) in pot. Salt to taste.

Cook until greens are tender and seasoning has permeated them. If any additional liquid is needed, add water. *Serves 8.*

Note: This recipe may also be used for fresh spinach or turnip greens.

"Don't forgot to drink the pot likker!"

"If you don' like mustard greens prepared in this way, you better call you' doctor quick an' fast, 'cause you is sick. Mos' bes' thing you can do is save that wondermous juice from this, put it in a cup, an' sneak back in the kitchen when no one is watchin' an' drink that you'self!

"This juice is call' pot likker, an' you' guests gonna wonder how come you come out of that kitchen lickin' you' chops all the time."

Okra's Origins

When the African slaves brought okra with them to the plantations of the South, they called the green vegetable "gumbo," and that word came into general use as the name of a stew or soup. Okra helps thicken whatever you want to cook it in.

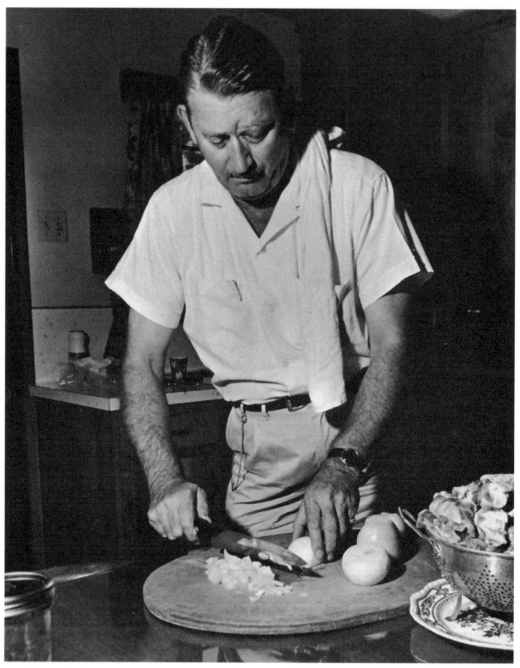

*Me and them onion, we got us a—how-you-call it—affinity. Me, I ain' shed my
firs' tear, 'til yet.* (Photo by Bill Cooksey)

CUT OKRA AND TOMATOES AU VIN

2 tbsp. olive oil
6 slices thick bacon, cubed
2 medium onions, chopped
  fine
1 clove garlic, minced
2 lb. fresh-cut okra
4 medium tomatoes, cut into 6
  or 8 pieces each

1 cup Sauterne wine or dry
  white wine
1 or 2 tsp. Louisiana hot sauce
1 tbsp. Worcestershire sauce
Salt

Put olive oil in a skillet large enough so that mixture can be stirred. Add cubed bacon, onions, and minced garlic. Sauté this for about 10 minutes. Add okra and tomatoes.

Pour wine over this, and add hot sauce and Worcestershire sauce. Salt to taste. Cook until okra is tender and has lost its green taste. *Serves 8.*

BOILED OKRA

2 lb. fresh young okra
½ cup olive oil
2 cups Sauterne wine or dry
  white wine

1 cup water
2 tsp. Louisiana hot sauce
2 tsp. salt

Wash okra well.

Put olive oil in pot, then add the okra. Pour wine and water over it, and add Louisiana hot sauce and salt.

Bring to a good boil, and then turn fire down and cook slowly until okra is tender. *Serves 8.*

One thing to remember: leave a small portion of stem on okra. This keeps it from gettin' slickery.

Okra Succotash

1 cup onion, chopped
1 cup bell pepper (and hot
   pepper if you have it),
   chopped
1 tbsp. garlic, chopped

3 cups okra, chopped
1 16-oz. can mashed tomatoes
1 16-oz. can creamed corn
Salt and pepper to taste

Put all ingredients in a big pot, and cook until the okra and onions are done.

Serve it over rice. *Serves 4-6.*

Irish Potatoes au Gratin au Vin

Olive oil
6 or 8 large potatoes, sliced
6 or 8 large onions, sliced
3 cups grated American and
   Parmesan or Romano cheese

Salt
Ground cayenne pepper
1 cup Sauterne wine or dry
   white wine

Preheat the oven to 375 degrees.

Cover bottom of casserole dish with olive oil, and rub the sides with it.

Place in the casserole dish a layer of sliced potatoes, then a layer of sliced onions, and a layer of cheese. Use at least two different types of cheese mixed together.

Sprinkle each layer with salt and cayenne pepper to taste. Repeat until casserole is full.

Pour wine over the whole mess, and bake in the preheated oven until tender.

"No doubt you notice this Irish potato recipe don' say how many it serves. Well, the reason that is is because you should ought to try this before you serve it to company. Chances is you gonna want to double the recipe when you see how good this is, I garontee! This will probably feed 6-8."

CAULIFLOWER OR BROCCOLI AU GRATIN

In the previous recipe, substitute cauliflower or broccoli for potatoes.

SQUASH DELIGHT

1 lb. sliced yellow squash	**½ cup mayonnaise**
½ cup green pepper, chopped	**½ cup margarine (if desired)**
½ cup celery, chopped	**Salt**
½ cup onion or green onions, chopped	**Cayenne pepper**
1 can water chestnuts, sliced	**½ cup grated American cheese**
	Bread crumbs

Preheat the oven to 325 degrees.

Boil sliced squash just until tender. Add the rest of the ingredients except bread crumbs.

Pour into a casserole dish, and top with bread crumbs and mix.

Bake in the preheated oven for 45 minutes. *Serves 4-8.*

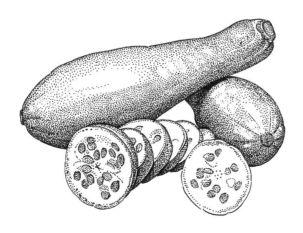

Squash and Shrimp

2 tbsp. olive oil
3 cups chopped onion
1 large banana pepper
  (or pickled hot pepper),
  chopped
1 cup chopped bell pepper
8 cups chopped squash (any
  kind)
1 cup Sauterne wine or dry
  white wine

1 cup dried shrimp
1 big clove garlic, minced
3 eggs, beaten well
Salt
Cayenne pepper
Bread crumbs
Parmesan cheese

Preheat the oven to 325 degrees.

Put the olive oil in a large pot. Sauté the onion, hot pepper, and bell pepper until clear.

Add the squash and wine. Cook until tender.

Stir in the shrimp and garlic, and cook 10 minutes.

Beat the eggs, and fold into the squash mixture. Add salt and pepper to taste.

Turn into a deep casserole dish. Top with bread crumbs and grated Parmesan cheese.

Bake in the preheated oven for 1 hour or until brown. *Serves 4-8.*

STEWED SQUASH AU VIN

3 to 4 lb. fresh young, tender
  squash
¼ lb. salt pork shoulder, lean
½ cup olive oil
3 large onions, chopped
1 chopped green hot pepper or
  1½ tsp. Louisiana hot sauce

2 small cloves garlic, diced or
  pressed
2 or 3 cups Sauterne wine or
  dry white wine
Salt
Water if needed

Peel and cut up squash.

Cube salt meat in ½-inch squares.

Pour olive oil in large cast-iron or heavy aluminum pot. Add the salt meat, and cook until soft, not brown.

Place squash, onions, pepper and garlic in pot. Pour wine over squash, and salt to taste.

Bring to a hard boil, and then lower fire and cook slowly until squash has lost its green taste and meat is tender, approximately 1 to 1½ hours. Add water if needed during cooking. *Serves 6-8.*

CACUSCA SQUASH CASSEROLE

1 cup chopped onion
8 cups sliced cacusca squash
½ cup chopped bell pepper
2 cloves garlic, chopped
1 tbsp. soy sauce
¼ tsp. bitters (Peychaud
  or Angostura)

1 tsp. Louisiana hot sauce
1 cup Sauterne wine or dry
  white wine
1 cup diced bacon
2 cups diced shrimp
Seasoned bread crumbs

Preheat the oven to 325 degrees.

Spray a casserole dish with nonstick cooking spray. Cook all of the ingredients together in a pot on top of the stove (except the bread crumbs) until the squash is tender.

Transfer to a casserole dish. Sprinkle seasoned bread crumbs on the top.

Bake in the preheated oven for 30 to 45 minutes. *Serves 6-8.*

CACUSCA STEW

1 medium cacusca squash,
   cut up
1 large bell pepper, chopped
3 ribs celery, chopped
2 large onions, chopped
1 bunch green onions,
   chopped
2 cloves garlic, chopped
½ lb. bacon, cut into pieces
4 cups diced potatoes

1 can Ro-Tel tomatoes
1 16-oz. can tomatoes
2 8-oz. cans tomato sauce
2 cups Sauterne wine or dry
   white wine
1 lb. fresh mushrooms, sliced
   or whole
1½ tsp. salt
2 tbsp. soy sauce
Water to cover well

Make a roux first if you want to. I like it better that way. (See my roux recipe.)

Mix all the ingredients together any damned way you want to, and bring to a boil. Simmer for 3 hours. *Serves 6-8.*

GREEN-TOMATO CASSEROLE À LA JUSTIN

2 tbsp. olive oil
6 green tomatoes, sliced thick
Onions (about 6 medium),
   sliced thin
Salt to taste

Seasoned salt to taste
½ cup Romano cheese, grated
3 tbsp. seasoned bread crumbs
2 slices bacon, sliced thick

Preheat the oven to 325 degrees.

Place a small amount of olive oil in a casserole with thick-sliced tomatoes, thin-sliced onions, salt, and seasoned salt. Add Romano cheese.

Repeat layers. Top with bread crumbs and sliced bacon.

Bake in the preheated oven for 1 hour. *Serves 4-6.*

FRIED GREEN TOMATOES

Olive oil or shortening
6 green tomatoes, sliced
½ cup cornmeal

¼ cup flour
Ground cayenne pepper
1 tsp. salt

Heat the oil in a frying pan over a high fire.
Blend the dry ingredients.
Roll the tomatoes in dry ingredients.
Fry the tomatoes in hot grease until golden brown on both sides.
Serves 4-6.

TURNIP CASSEROLE

10 cups cooked and mashed
  turnips
1 cup grated American cheese
1 cup tuna
1 cup chopped clams
1 cup chopped green onion
½ lb. diced bacon
2 cups seasoned bread crumbs

4 eggs, beaten
½ cup dried parsley
Salt to taste
1 tbsp. soy sauce
½ tsp. Louisiana hot sauce
½ cup Sauterne wine or dry
  white wine
½ tsp. garlic powder

Preheat the oven to 350 degrees.
Layer the turnips, cheese, tuna, clams, onions, bacon, and bread crumbs in a greased casserole dish. Make 2 layers.
Beat eggs, and blend in with the rest of the ingredients.
Pour this mixture over the layers in the dish.
Bake in the preheated oven until brown and tender. *Serves 8-10.*

SAUTÉED MUSHROOMS

3 lb. fresh mushrooms
Salted water
Water
2 tbsp. olive oil
1 stick margarine
1½ cups Sauterne wine or dry
   white wine

2 tbsp. soy sauce
½ tsp. cayenne pepper
1 tbsp. lime or lemon juice
1½ tsp. salt
½ tsp. garlic powder

Soak mushrooms in salted water, wash, and then soak them in fresh water. Drain.

Put 2 tbsp. olive oil in a skillet.

Add all the other ingredients, and sauté until the mushrooms are tender. *Serves 4-6.*

"And you talk about good! They'll give you indigestion, but they're mighty fine!"

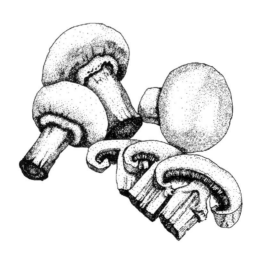

Baked Macaroni and Cheese au Vin

2 12-oz. pkg. macaroni
Olive oil
2½ cups grated American
   cheese, per layer
½ cup grated Romano cheese
Strip with Swiss cheese
6 eggs
2½ cups Sauterne wine or dry
   white wine

1½ tbsp. Worcestershire sauce
1½ tsp. green Louisiana hot
   sauce (red, if green is not
   available)
1½ tsp. salt
Water if needed

Preheat the oven to 350 degrees.

Cook macaroni, drain in colander, wash with cold water.

Grease casserole dish with olive oil, including sides and bottom.

This casserole is made in layers. Start with macaroni, add cheeses, and add another layer of macaroni and another topping with cheese until casserole is full.

Beat eggs, add wine to beaten eggs, add Worcestershire to this mixture, and add green Louisiana hot sauce and salt.

Pour this over layered casserole, and add water, if necessary, to barely cover.

Bake in preheated oven until top layer of cheese is golden brown. *Serves 8.*

Suggestion: If any of this is left over—and that ain't likely—chill, cut like fudge, and serve as hors d'oeuvres the next day or so.

"Here's where you' nose come in handy. When you mixes that wine wit' them egg, you gonna know it's right when the mixture done smell jus' like eggnog at Chris'mus time. But don' drink it, no, you! Put it in the recipe, jus' like I tol' you."

Rhody Macaroni

1 cup macaroni	Milk
1 tbsp. butter or margarine	1 egg, beaten
4 oz. cheddar cheese	1 cup milk
4 oz. mushroom pieces	Salt
Saltine crackers	Pepper

Preheat the oven to about 350 degrees.

Cook the macaroni 7 minutes, drain and rinse under cold water, and set aside.

Select a baking pan of 1-quart capacity. Warm and line with the butter.

Put ⅓ of the macaroni in the pan, grate or slice some cheddar cheese over the macaroni, add 1 tablespoon of the mushroom pieces and 6 saltines, and cover with milk.

Continue adding the same layers until all of these ingredients are used.

Add one beaten egg to the 1 cup of milk, and put on the second layer.

Top off with a few bits of cheese, which will brown and give a bit of color.

Bake, uncovered, in a moderate oven until brown and bubbly. *Serves 6-8.*

Note: Be sure that the milk covers the entire surface of this dish before placing it in the oven. Salt and pepper should be used to taste about the middle of the assembly. Quantities of cheese and mushrooms may be used to suit your taste. Cooking time is governed by the depth of the pan, but usually a spoon test should be made after 25 minutes.

LEFTOVERS

*Look, ma frien'. Don' argue wit' me about what we got cooked. Taste it an'
see if it don' taste jus' like I tol' you it would.* (Photo by David King
Gleason)

LEFTOVER SPAGHETTI CASSEROLE I

Whenever you cook spaghetti, you can put anything you want in the leftovers to make a casserole. This is your chance to be creative.

Spaghetti, cooked
Olive oil
American cheese, grated
Swiss cheese, grated
Romano cheese, grated
Dried parsley
Butter-flavored salt
¼ tsp. bitters (Peychaud or Angostura)

1 tbsp. Worcestershire sauce or soy sauce
1 tsp. Louisiana hot sauce
2 cups Sauterne wine or dry white wine
6 eggs
Bacon, sliced

Grease a casserole dish with olive oil.

Put a layer of leftover spaghetti and a layer of three cheeses, and sprinkle some dried parsley on top.

Add salt, bitters, Worcestershire sauce and hot sauce to the wine, and beat together with the eggs. Pour all over the whole thing.

Take sliced bacon, and strip it on the top.

Bake at 325 degrees until the bacon is done. *Serves 6-8.*

"Dat's what you call a 'musgo' casserole. It mus' go down!"

What kinda wine to drink wit' dis fine food? Why, hell, the kind dat you likes the bes', dat's the kind. (Photo by David King Gleason)

LEFTOVER SPAGHETTI CASSEROLE II

Use the same ingredients as Leftover Spaghetti Casserole I, and add 2 pounds peeled shrimp.

Make two layers, one with spaghetti and one with shrimp and cheese.

Put all of the seasonings in the wine, and mix with the eggs. Pour over the layers.

Add 1 cup seasoned bread crumbs on the top of this one.

Bake at 325 degrees until bacon is done.

1 16-oz. can Ro-Tel tomatoes may be used instead of wine for both. *Serves 6-8.*

LEFTOVER MACARONI AND CHEESE

Slice leftover macaroni in 1-inch slices. Put on a bed of lettuce. Top with mayonnaise and paprika, and have a nice salad.

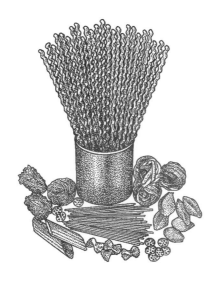

Ham Kabob with Rice Salad

1 cup uncooked brown rice
2 cups water
1 tsp. salt
¼ cup bottled clear French
   dressing
1 tbsp. honey
½ cup finely diced celery
2 tbsp. sliced green onions or
   scallions

2 tbsp. canned pimiento,
   chopped
2 tbsp. mayonnaise
Crisp lettuce leaves
32 1-inch cubes leftover ham
24 honeydew melon balls
8 maraschino cherries (optional)

In a heavy 1½-quart saucepan, combine rice, water, and salt. Place over moderately high heat (about 275 degrees), and bring to a full boil. Reduce heat to moderately low (about 225 degrees), and cover pan tightly. Cook 40-45 minutes, or until the rice is tender and all of the liquid is absorbed.

Turn the rice into a large bowl, and stir in French dressing and honey. Cover and chill in the refrigerator about 1 hour. When the rice is cold, add the celery, onions, pimiento, and mayonnaise.

Spoon equal amounts of the rice salad onto each of four lettuce-lined plates. On each of eight wooden skewers, arrange alternately four ham cubes and three melon balls. End with a cherry if desired. Place two kabobs on each plate with the salad. *Serves 4.*

TURKEY HASH

½ cup flour
1½ tbsp. bacon drippings or cooking oil
3 cups chopped onion
2 cups chopped celery
1 cup chopped bell pepper
1 cup parsley, chopped
2 cups green onions or shallots, chopped
1 tbsp. garlic, chopped
½ large lemon, chopped
½ tsp. dried mint
¼ tsp. bitters (Peychaud or Angostura)
3 tbsp. Worcestershire sauce
2 tsp. Louisiana hot sauce or 1 tsp. Tabasco sauce
1 cup chopped carrots
3 cups chopped Irish potatoes
Water if needed
6 cups leftover turkey (at least)
1 cup Sauterne wine or dry white wine
Salt

Preheat the oven to 325 or 350 degrees.

Make a roux with the flour and bacon drippings. (See my roux recipe.) Add chopped onion, celery, and bell pepper after the roux is browned. Simmer until the vegetables are clear or tender.

Stir in the chopped parsley, green onions, and garlic, and simmer until tender.

Add lemon, dried mint, bitters, Worcestershire sauce, hot sauce, carrots, potatoes, and a little water. Simmer for 15 minutes.

Pour the mixture into a baking pan. Add the turkey, wine, and enough water to not quite cover. Salt to taste. Bake in the preheated oven until brown and not quite dry. *Serves 6-8.*

Variation: You can use the same ingredients to make hash out of any kind of roast (beef, pork, venison). But for these, increase the dried mint to 1 teaspoon. The mint brings out the flavor of the meat.

"After you make dis turkey hash, you can't look another turkey in the face 'til nex' Thanksgiving. Dat's for true, I garontee!"

Ham Soufflé

¼ cup butter or margarine
¼ cup finely chopped onion
¼ cup flour
1 cup milk
½ cup grated sharp cheddar
    cheese
½ tsp. Worcestershire sauce

¼ tsp. salt
¼ tsp. dry mustard
5 eggs, at room temperature
    (separate yolks and whites)
1 tbsp. chopped fresh parsley
1½ cups finely diced or
    chopped leftover baked ham

Preheat oven to 350 degrees.

In a small saucepan over moderate heat (about 250 degrees), melt the butter.

Add the onion, and cook until tender. Quickly stir in the flour, and blend until smooth. (A wire whip is helpful.) Heat until the flour mixture is bubbly.

Remove the pan from the heat, and gradually stir in the milk. Return the mixture to heat, and bring to a boil, stirring constantly.

Add cheese, Worcestershire sauce, salt, and mustard; cook, stirring constantly, until cheese melts. Remove the pan from the heat.

In a large bowl, slightly beat the egg yolks. Gradually stir the hot cheese mixture into the yolks; blend smooth. Stir in parsley and ham.

Beat the egg whites until stiff, but not dry. Fold the egg whites into the ham mixture.

Turn the mixture into an ungreased 2-quart soufflé dish.

Bake in the preheated oven 45 minutes, or until a knife inserted in the center comes out clean. Serve immediately. *Serves 4-6.*

Lamb Salad

1½ cups diced leftover roast
lamb
2 tbsp. bottled clear French
dressing
1 tbsp. lemon juice
½ cup diced celery
¼ cup chopped bell pepper
1 tbsp. chopped onion
1 tbsp. canned pimiento,
chopped

1 tbsp. drained capers
¼ cup mayonnaise
2 tbsp. crumbled bleu cheese
¼ tsp. dried mint
¼ tsp. garlic salt
Dash Louisiana hot sauce
Crisp lettuce leaves
Fresh parsley sprigs

In a bowl, combine lamb, French dressing, and lemon juice.

Add celery, bell pepper, onion, pimiento, and capers to the lamb mixture. Set aside while preparing remaining ingredients. Stir occasionally.

Mix together in a small bowl the mayonnaise, bleu cheese, mint, garlic salt, and hot sauce. Stir into the lamb mixture.

Spoon equal amounts of the salad onto two or three lettuce-lined plates. Garnish with parsley. *Serves 2-3.*

Dat's a dude, I garontee! (Photo by David King Gleason)

BREADS, BISCUITS, AND DUMPLINGS

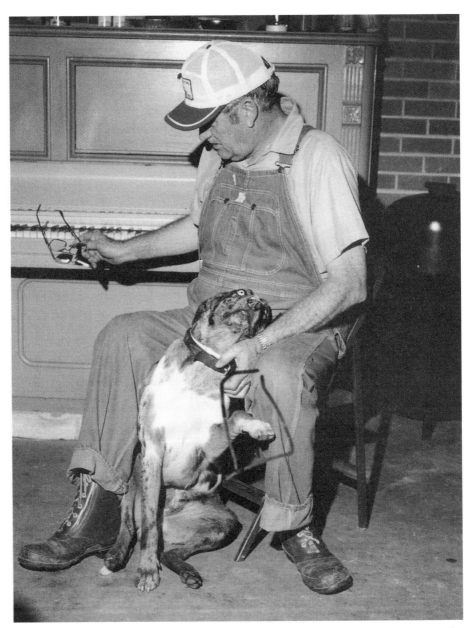

Look at the love that dog has in his eyes for me. He was a Catahoula named Chien, which means "dog" in French. (Photo by David King Gleason)

Hush Puppies

1 cup cornmeal
½ cup flour
1 tsp. baking powder
1 tsp. salt
½ tsp. soda

1 egg, beaten
1 medium onion, finely
   chopped
¾ to 1 cup milk or buttermilk

Combine all dry ingredients. Add egg, milk, and onions. Mix well. Drop in deep hot fat by spoonfuls and brown on all sides. *Makes 8-10.*

Maxine's French Bread

1 qt. warm water
3 2-oz. pkg. yeast
3 tsp. salt

2 tsp. lard or shortening
6 tbsp. sugar
11 cups flour

Mix all of the ingredients in the water, adding the flour last. Let the dough rise 1 hour.

Knead, mold into a long French-bread loaf, and let stand another ½ hour. Preheat the oven to 400 degrees.

Bake in the preheated oven until brown.

Homemade Rolls à la Rosina

3 pkg. dry yeast
½ cup lukewarm water (must
    not be hot)
1½ cups warm milk (not hot)

4 tbsp. cooking oil
1 tbsp. salt
2 tbsp. sugar
5 or 6 cups of all-purpose flour

Dissolve yeast in water. Add milk, oil, salt, and sugar. Stir until sugar and salt dissolve.

Put flour into a medium-sized mixing bowl, pour the liquid mixture into flour, and stir until dough becomes rather stiff. Knead by hand until dough is stiff.

Put the dough in a greased bowl, grease top of dough, set in a warm place, and let it rise until it is at least double in size (about 45 minutes).

Flour your bread board, remove dough from bowl to board, and knead down.

Pinch off small pieces of dough. Shape into rolls, and put on a greased cookie sheet. Lightly grease the top of each roll.

Set them in a warm place, and let the rolls rise for approximately 35 minutes. Preheat oven to 475 degrees.

Place the pans on the oven rack and bake until golden brown (about 15 minutes). *Makes 40 rolls.*

Hot Water Corn Bread

1 cup cornmeal
½ cup flour

1 tsp. salt
Boiling water

Blend dry ingredients.

Add boiling water to make a very stiff batter.

Using a spoon, make small pones, and drop in deep hot grease until brown on all sides.

CORN BREAD

2 tbsp. shortening
1½ cups yellow cornmeal
1 cup flour
3 tsp. baking powder

1 tsp. salt
2 eggs
1 cup milk

Preheat the oven to 350 degrees.

Heat the shortening in a skillet.

Mix the dry ingredients well.

Beat the eggs, and blend in with dry ingredients.

Add milk to reach desired consistency (not too runny).

Pour the shortening from the hot skillet into the batter, and beat real good.

Bake in the preheated oven until brown.

When brown, take the corn bread out of the oven, and flip it over to sweat it. If you don't, it will mildew.

Turn the oven off. Place the corn bread back in the skillet, and keep warm in the oven.

Me, I got a frien'. Pete his front name, Fountain his behin' name. (Photo by Bill Cooksey)

Mexican Corn Bread

1 cup flour
1½ cups cornmeal
3 tsp. baking powder
1 tsp. salt
½ tsp. soda
1 tsp. sugar
1 11-oz. can whole-kernel corn

2 eggs
2 jalapeno peppers, chopped
2 tbsp. chopped bell pepper
1 cup sour cream or buttermilk
½ cup bacon drippings
1 cup grated American cheese

Preheat the oven to 350 degrees.

Mix all of the ingredients together except the bacon drippings and cheese.

Heat the bacon drippings in a skillet and pour in half of the mixture.

Sprinkle half of the cheese on the top, then add the rest of the mixture and the remaining cheese. Bake in the preheated oven for 45 minutes.

Cornpone

1 cup yellow cornmeal
   (home-ground if possible)
¾ cup plain flour
1 tsp. salt
2 tsp. baking powder

½ tsp. onion powder
¼ tsp. garlic powder
1 cup milk (maybe more)
2 eggs

Mix the dry ingredients. Add some of the milk until you can work the batter.

Beat the eggs, and add to the batter. Make batter thin enough to fry, just like you would pancakes. Remember, if you want thick cornpone cakes, you must have thick batter.

Spoon batter onto a hot, greased griddle, and fry for about 15 minutes or until lightly browned. *Serves 4-6.*

"These are good, and something else about them: They can be fixed real quick, so you can have cornpone with greens or whatever you want to have it with. Also, too, be sure an' butter 'em real good."

CORN BREAD DRESSING

1 loaf toasted corn bread	Salt and pepper to taste
6 cups finely chopped celery	10 cups hot stock (chicken or
6 cups finely chopped onion	turkey)
6 raw eggs, well beaten	Enough hot water to make
12 slices toast, crumbled	heavy mixture
1 tsp. sage	

Bake the corn bread until brown. (See my recipe). Turn the oven down to 325 degrees.

Stir all of the ingredients together with the corn bread, and pour into a baking pan.

Bake at 325 degrees for approximately 1½ hours or until brown. *Serves 6-10.*

"You can check dis like a cake."

BISCUITS

2 cups all-purpose flour	½ tsp. baking soda
3 tsp. baking powder	2 tbsp. shortening
½ tsp. salt	1¼ cups buttermilk

Preheat the oven to 475 degrees.

Sift the dry ingredients together. Blend in the shortening and buttermilk, and mix well.

Roll the biscuit dough out on waxed paper covered with flour.

Cut out biscuits with a biscuit cutter, or pinch them off, and place them in a greased pan.

Bake in the preheated oven for about 15 minutes.

SOURDOUGH BISCUITS

1 pkg. yeast
1 cup warm water
2 cups buttermilk
½ cup sugar
4 tsp. baking powder

½ cup cooking oil
1 tsp. salt
¼ tsp. soda
5 cups flour (maybe more)

Dissolve yeast in water. Mix together thoroughly with all of the ingredients except flour. Add 5 or more cups of flour and mix well.

Put the dough in a covered bowl in the refrigerator for 12 hours or more before using.

When ready to bake, preheat the oven to 450 degrees, roll out the dough, and pinch off biscuits.

Bake in a greased pan in the preheated oven until golden brown.

MARTHA'S BEER BISCUITS

2 cups Bisquick all-purpose
   baking mix
½ cup finely chopped green
   onions

½ cup grated cheddar cheese
2 tbsp. shortening
Beer

Preheat the oven to 450 degrees.

Mix together the Bisquick, onion, and cheese. Cut the shortening into the mixture, and add enough beer to make the dough slightly stiff.

Turn out onto a Bisquick-covered board. Knead a few times, and cut into individual biscuits.

Bake in the preheated oven until browned.

Me, I don' cook all the time. Sometime I gotta work at bein' a safety engineer, too. (Photo by Bill Cooksey)

REFRIGERATOR BISCUITS

1 pkg. dry yeast
¼ cup warm water
5 cups self-rising flour
1 tsp. soda

1 cup Crisco shortening
2 cups buttermilk

Dissolve the yeast in warm water, and set aside.

Mix the other ingredients, and add to the yeast mixture. Knead dough on a floured board until smooth.

You can make some biscuits now, and store the rest of the dough in a plastic bag in the refrigerator. No rising is required before baking. Bake as many as you want when you want them. The longer the dough stays in the refrigerator, the better the biscuits.

Preheat the oven to 400 degrees. Cut biscuits out or pinch the dough off into biscuits and bake them until done. Make very small biscuits because they double in size while baking.

POTATO KLÖSSE

2 lb. boiled potatoes
1 tbsp. finely chopped onion
1 tbsp. finely chopped parsley
1 tbsp. butter
2-3 tbsp. flour (or more)

2 eggs, beaten
Salt
1½ slices toasted bread, crumbled
3 qt. salted, boiling water

Either mash or grate the potatoes.

Simmer the onions, parsley, and butter and mix well with the potatoes and flour.

Add the eggs, salt, and bread crumbs. Make smooth round balls. (Flour your hands before making balls.)

Place the potato balls in the boiling water, and simmer for 8 to 10 minutes.

Dumplings for Chicken or Anything Else

2 cups all-purpose flour
¾ tsp. salt
3 tsp. baking powder

2 tbsp. bacon drippings
1 cup (scant) cold bouillon or
   meat stock

Sift together the flour, salt, and baking powder. Cut in the bacon drippings.

Moisten with the broth to make a drop batter.

Drop the dumplings by teaspoonfuls into boiling soup or stock. Cover and steam for 12 minutes.

Brunch Yam Bread

1 1-lb. can Louisiana yams in
   orange-pineapple sauce
¾ cup sauce from yams
1 tbsp. lemon juice
1 tsp. grated lemon rind
2 eggs

2½ cups biscuit mix
1 tsp. cinnamon
½ tsp. nutmeg
¼ tsp. allspice
½ cup milk

Preheat the oven to 350 degrees.

Place the yams and sauce in a mixing bowl and mash well. Stir in lemon juice and rind; beat in eggs. Add the biscuit mix and spices and beat well. Stir in milk.

Spoon the batter into a greased loaf pan (9-by-5-by-3-inch).

Bake in the preheated oven for 55 to 65 minutes. Turn out on a rack to cool. Slice and serve warm with butter. *Serves 4-6.*

Date and Nut Bread

2 cups apple cider
2 cups chopped and pitted
    dates
⅔ cup soft butter or margarine
2 cups granulated sugar
2 eggs

3 cups sifted flour
2 tsp. baking soda
⅛ tsp. salt
1 tsp. vanilla
2 cups chopped nuts

Preheat the oven to 275 degrees.

Bring the apple cider to a boil, and pour over the dates. Set aside.

Cream butter or margarine and sugar together. Add eggs, and mix thoroughly.

Sift together the flour, soda, and salt, and add to the creamed mixture alternately with vanilla and the cider-date mixture. Add the nuts.

Grease and flour two loaf pans and divide dough equally between them.

Bake in the preheated oven for 1 hour and 45 minutes. While still warm, wrap each loaf in waxed paper, and then a clean tea towel. *Serves 6-8.*

This is me on a rocket, and I didn't get far, no! (Photo illustration by David King Gleason)

Sauces,
Salad Dressings,
Pickles,
and Jellies

Don' start dat foolishment wit' me. Dat's the one I want, not the one you got in your hand over dare. Can't you see where I'm pointin', where ma finger's at rat on it dare, hanh? (Photo by David King Gleason)

Bordelaise Sauce à la Sara

¼ lb. margarine or butter
½ cup chopped mushrooms
1 tbsp. finely chopped parsley
½ tsp. Louisiana hot sauce
1 tbsp. soy sauce

2 tbsp. lemon juice
½ tsp. finely chopped garlic
1 tbsp. Sauterne wine or dry
   white wine

Sauté the mushrooms and parsley in butter or margarine.

Add the hot sauce, soy sauce, lemon juice, and garlic. Finish with Sauterne or dry white wine. Cook for 15-20 minutes.

Serve over steak or chops.

Cajunized Chinese Sauce

1 tsp. Worcestershire sauce
½ tsp. onion powder
¼ tsp. garlic powder
1 tbsp. soy sauce
1 tsp. lemon-pepper seasoning
½ tsp. bitters (Peychaud or
   Angostura)

½ cup Sauterne wine or dry
   white wine
Hot peppers, cut into strips
Bell peppers, cut into strips
Olive oil
Chicken, beef, or pork, cut up

Preheat the oven to 325 or 350 degrees.

Mix the Worcestershire sauce, onion powder, garlic powder, soy sauce, lemon pepper, bitters, and wine with the pepper strips.

Grease a baking pan with olive oil, place the meat in it, and pour the sauce over the whole doggone thing.

Bake in the preheated oven until your meat is done.

SHRIMP DIP

(DIPPING SAUCE FOR BOILED SHRIMP)

1 can tomato soup
½ cup catsup
4 tsp. Louisiana hot sauce
½ tsp. onion juice
¼ tsp. garlic salt

½ tsp. minced celery
Dash paprika
Dash cayenne pepper
2 tbsp. creamed butter

Combine all of the ingredients, except butter, and whip together well. Chill.

Just before serving, blend in the butter until the mixture becomes smooth. Use for dunking shrimp.

REMOULADE SAUCE À LA JUSTIN

1 gal. mayonnaise
2½ cups Dijon mustard
2½ cups Durkee's Famous
　Sauce
2 cups horseradish
2 tsp. salt

¾ cup Louisiana hot sauce
½ small bottle Worcestershire
　sauce
1 tsp. cayenne pepper
1 tsp. celery salt

Thoroughly mix all of the ingredients together. Chill, and serve with peeled boiled shrimp.

"Make a lot and keep it in the refrigerator. The sauce will keep indefinitely. And it's delicious, especially when poured over boiled shrimp to make Shrimp Remoulade!"

Slaw Dressing

½ cup sugar
¼ cup vinegar
1 tsp. dry mustard
1 tsp. salt
½ tsp. cayenne pepper

1 cup mayonnaise
1 cup olive oil
1 tsp. celery seed
1 tbsp. lemon juice

Cook the sugar, vinegar, mustard, salt, and cayenne pepper for 15-20 minutes. Remove from fire, and let cool.

Add mayonnaise. Beat in the oil slowly. Add celery seed, lemon juice, and more salt (if necessary), and mix thoroughly.

Combine with cole slaw for a very tasty slaw! *Makes about 3 cups of dressing.*

Honey Dressing

¼ cup sugar
1 tsp. dry mustard
1 tsp. paprika
1 tsp. celery seed
1 tsp. salt

⅓ cup vinegar
⅓ cup honey
1 tbsp. lemon juice
Onion juice, if desired
1 cup salad oil

Beat all of the ingredients except the oil in a small mixing bowl.

Add the oil slowly, beating constantly. *Makes about 2 cups of dressing.*

"This dressing is good for slaw or for fruit salads. If you leave the salad oil out, this can also be used as a sweet-and-sour sauce."

Mermaid Sauce

1 pt. salad dressing
1 tsp. chopped garlic
½ cup Sauterne wine or dry
    white wine

1 tsp. salt
2 tsp. Louisiana hot sauce
2 tsp. Worcestershire sauce
2 tsp. honey

Mix all of the ingredients together. Chill and use over a green salad.

Cooked Barbecue Sauce

4 tbsp. olive oil
2 medium onions
2 cloves garlic
½ cup parsley
1 small cayenne pepper,
    pickled or fresh (if not
    available, ½-¾ tsp. Louisiana
    hot sauce)

1 cup Sauterne wine or dry
    white wine
1 tbsp. lemon juice
2 tbsp. Worcestershire sauce
1½ tsp. salt
1 tsp. Liquid Smoke
1 small can tomato sauce

Heat olive oil in large saucepan.

Put onions, garlic, parsley, and hot pepper in a blender. If you don't have a blender, chop really fine.

Blend, with just enough water to make it blend.

Pour into the saucepan, and cook over low flame for about 30 minutes.

Add wine, lemon juice, Worcestershire sauce, salt, Liquid Smoke, and tomato sauce.

Cover and simmer this entire mixture until onions are done, about 1 hour, maybe a few minutes more. If needed, add water.

"One of the mos' bes' things about this barbecue sauce is the onions in it. An' you say to me, 'How I gonna know when a onion is done?' an' I gonna told you real quick, 'When it don' taste like a raw onion, tha's when!' In other words, a onion is done when it is sof' and tender, not crunchy."

BARBECUE SAUCE WITH ADDED COMMERCIAL BARBECUE SAUCE

4 tbsp. olive oil
4 cups chopped onions (dry onions)
2 cloves garlic
½ cup parsley
2 tsp. Louisiana hot sauce
1 cup Sauterne wine or dry white wine

1 tbsp. lemon juice
2 tsp. Worcestershire sauce
1 cup water
1 tsp. Liquid Smoke
1 qt. commercial barbecue sauce

Heat olive oil in large saucepan.

Put onions, garlic, parsley, and hot sauce in a blender. If you don't have a blender, chop really fine.

Blend, with just enough water to make it blend.

Pour into the saucepan, and cook over low flame for about 30 minutes.

Add wine, lemon juice, Worcestershire sauce, water, and Liquid Smoke.

Cover and simmer this entire mixture for 30 minutes.

Add 1 qt. of commercial barbecue sauce. Simmer for 1 hour. *Makes 6-8 cups of sauce.*

SAWMILL GRAVY

Sawmill Gravy can be made from grease in which chicken, rabbit, or round steak has been fried.

1 cup grease   **Salt**
Flour   **Pepper**
Milk

Pour off all but 1 cup of the grease, but leave crumbs.

Add enough flour to take up all grease, and brown to deep brown.

Add milk to make thin gravy, stirring constantly. Salt and pepper to taste.

Cook until thickened, and serve over bread, corn bread, or rice. More milk can be added if it thickens too much. *Makes about 2 cups of gravy.*

CHOW CHOW

1 gal. green tomatoes   **1 tsp. cloves**
½ cup salt   **1 cup sugar**
1 head cabbage   **2-3 garlic cloves, finely**
4 large onions   **chopped**
1 tsp. allspice   **2-3 hot green peppers**
1 tsp. cinnamon   **1 qt. vinegar**

Chop the tomatoes, and place in a crock pot or large enamel bowl. Add ½ cup salt, and stir. Let it sit overnight.

The next day, soak tomatoes, cabbage, and onions all together for 2 hours. Drain off the juice and pour vegetables into large cooking pot.

Add allspice, cinnamon, cloves, sugar, garlic, and hot peppers.

Pour in enough vinegar to boil (about 1 quart). Cook until the tomatoes are tender.

Place the mixture in sterilized jars while it's hot, and seal. (Taste for salt. If it's too salty, rinse before you place in jars.) *Makes about 4 quarts or 8 pints of chow chow.*

PEPPER JELLY

1 pt. apple jelly   ½ tsp. chopped hot pepper
1 tbsp. finely chopped bell
  pepper

Over low heat, slowly melt one pint of apple jelly.
To the melted jelly, add the bell pepper and hot pepper.
Pour the mixture back into the jar, and cover. *Makes 1 pint.*

"For color, use combined red and green pepper. To make jelly more spicy, use more pepper to taste."

GINA'S RELISH

1 doz. green bell peppers   1 tsp. salt
1 doz. red bell peppers   1 tsp. celery salt
10 medium onions   2 cups sugar
3 cups vinegar   1 tbsp. ground cloves

Grind the peppers and onions.
Put in a colander; pour boiling water over, stirring well. Let drain.
Put the mixture in a pot, and again pour boiling water over. Let it stand 10 minutes, then drain well.
Mix the vinegar, salt, celery salt, sugar, and cloves.
Add to the relish, and boil for 20 to 25 minutes. Chill and serve as a side dish.

Note: Two bushels of peppers make 8 bushels cooked. Use approximately 2 quarts of vinegar, 20 pounds of onions, and 20 pounds of sugar to make 47 pints.

Pickled Sweet Mirliton

⅓ cup vinegar
¼ cup beet juice
⅓ cup sugar
¼ tsp. whole allspice
1 stick whole cinnamon per jar

1/16 tsp. whole cloves
⅛ tsp. salt
1 pt. raw, sliced mirliton (⅛- to
    ¼-inch-thick slices)

Combine the vinegar, beet juice, sugar, spices, and salt.

Bring to a boil, then simmer 15 minutes. Add mirliton slices, and simmer 5 minutes.

Pack hot slices into hot, sterilized jars.

Bring syrup back to a boil, and pour over the mirliton. If not enough to cover, add hot vinegar. Seal immediately. *Makes about 2 pints.*

"You can do anyt'ing you want to wit' mirliton, an' it will taste good. As a matter of fact, mirliton can do mos' anyt'ing but drive a car!"

APPLE BUTTER

12 large cooking apples
1 qt. water
2 cups Sauterne wine or dry
  white wine
5 cups sugar (or more)

6 cups apple cider
2 tsp. cinnamon
2 tsp. ground cloves
1 tsp. allspice

Wash, quarter, and core apples.

Cook in water and wine until soft, about 10 minutes. (If using a blender to mash cooked apples, peel apples before cooking.)

Force the mixture through a sieve or food mill, discarding the skins. Add half as much sugar as you have pulp.

In a large saucepan, heat cider to boiling. Add the apple mixture, and cook over medium heat until 1 teaspoon of the apple mixture dropped onto a cold plate will hold its shape.

Stir the mixture often to prevent sticking and add spices as it thickens. *Makes 4 pints.*

"Apple Butter thickens when chilled. The mixture should be thick enough to spread."

It don' make t'ings taste more better, but sometime me, I jus' gotta dress the part, too. (Photo by Bill Cooksey)

DESSERTS

My first cookbook didn't include any desserts for two ver' good reasons, I garontee!

In the firstes' place, me I don' like desserts very much at all.

In the secondes' place, me, I sure don' need no desserts, or I'm gonna be big as a house sometime soon.

But mos'ly, you don' got no place some at all to put a dessert after you eat a real Cajun meal!

You gonna get you' plumb satisfy jus' eatin' what's in this cookbook.

Anyone what wants a dessert, me, I tell them that the mos' bes' thing they can eat for dessert is maybe a little sherbet or a dip of ice cream wit' a tablespoon of wine or brandy on top. Me, I'm real partial to a bowl of vanilla ice cream with a cup of amaretta liqueur on the side—you know, to pour over it. There just ain't nothin' better, I garontee!

If you just gotta have somethin' sweet after you' dinner, you' gonna love these for sure!

PUMPKIN PIE WITH
PRALINE TOPPING À LA MAXINE

PUMPKIN PIE

2 eggs
1 1-lb. can pumpkin
¾ cup firmly packed light
   brown sugar
½ tsp. salt

1½ tsp. pumpkin pie spice
1 tall can (1⅔ cups) evaporated
   milk
1 9-inch unbaked pie shell
Praline Topping

Preheat the oven to 400 degrees.

In a medium-sized mixing bowl, beat the eggs slightly. Stir in pumpkin, brown sugar, salt, spice, and evaporated milk, mixing well.

Pour most of the filling into the pastry shell, then place the pie on the oven rack. Carefully pour in the rest of the filling. (This helps to keep from spilling.)

Bake in the preheated oven (400 degrees) for 15 minutes; turn oven temperature down to moderate (350 degrees), and continue baking 45 minutes longer, or until the filling is done when tested.

Cool pie slightly, then refrigerate until serving time.

When ready to serve, make Praline Topping, and sprinkle evenly over pie.

Place the pie under broiler heat until the topping is bubbly (about 1 minute), watching carefully so that the mixture does not burn. Serve at once. *Makes one 9-inch pie.*

PRALINE TOPPING

2 tbsp. margarine
½ cup firmly packed light
   brown sugar

⅓ cup chopped pecans
   (peanuts or walnuts may be
   used instead)

Melt the margarine in a small saucepan. Remove from heat.
Stir in brown sugar and pecans.
Pour over Pumpkin Pie.

This li'l booney-cat Cajun already can count hisself up to twenty in French! (Photo by Bill Cooksey)

LOUISIANA PECAN PIE

3 eggs
1 cup brown or white sugar
1 cup corn syrup
1 tsp. butter
3 tbsp. flour

½ tsp. salt
1 tsp. vanilla
2 cups pecan meats
1 9-inch pie crust

Preheat the oven to 350 degrees.

Beat the eggs. Add sugar, syrup, butter, flour, salt, vanilla, and pecans.

Pour into a pie crust that has been baked for a few minutes (long enough to dry it out).

Bake in the preheated oven for about 1 hour or until the pie is firm in the middle. *Makes one 9-inch pie.*

LEMON PIE

1 can condensed milk
1 can lemonade frozen
  concentrate
1 large container Cool Whip
  topping

Graham-cracker pie crust (or
  vanilla wafers)

Mix condensed milk, frozen lemonade, and Cool Whip topping together, and pour into graham-cracker crust or over vanilla wafers. Garnish with additional Cool Whip if you desire. Chill for 2 hours. Leftovers should be refrigerated. *Makes 1 pie.*

Shoo-Fly Pie

¾ cup unsifted flour	2 tbsp. butter or shortening
½ tsp. cinnamon	1½ tsp. baking soda
⅛ tsp. ground nutmeg	¾ cup boiling water
⅛ tsp. ground cloves	½ cup light molasses
½ cup sugar	1 egg, well beaten
½ tsp. salt	1 pastry for a 9-inch pie

Preheat the oven to 400 degrees.

In a medium bowl, combine flour, cinnamon, nutmeg, and cloves. Add sugar and salt.

Cut in the butter with a pastry knife or with 2 knives until the mixture resembles coarse meal.

Dissolve baking soda in boiling water. Add molasses and egg, and blend well.

Line a 9-inch pie plate with pastry; shape edges. Pour half of the liquid into the pastry shell.

Add ¼ of the flour mixture, and stir gently.

Pour in the rest of the liquid, and top evenly with the remaining flour mixture.

Bake in the preheated oven for 10 minutes. Reduce heat to 325 degrees, and bake until the pie is set and the crust is golden (about 25 minutes). *Makes 1 pie.*

JIFFY GEL SUNDAES

1 3-oz. pkg. black cherry flavored gelatin
⅔ cup boiling water

1 qt. vanilla ice cream or pineapple sherbet

Empty the flavored gelatin into a medium bowl. Add ⅔ cup boiling water, and stir until the gelatin is dissolved.

Divide the ice cream or sherbet among eight dessert dishes.

Spoon the hot gelatin mixture over ice cream. The cherry sauce thickens as it touches the ice cream. *Serves 8.*

"Try your own favorite flavors of flavored gelatin and ice cream for a rainbow of sundae toppings."

FRUITCAKE COOKIES

1 stick butter or margarine
1½ cups packed dark brown sugar
4 eggs
1 cup claret wine
3 tbsp. sweet milk
1 tsp. rum extract
3 cups flour
2 tsp. soda

1 tsp. cinnamon
1 tsp. cloves
1 tsp. allspice
1 tsp. nutmeg
2 lb. candied cherries
2 lb. candied pineapple
2 lb. mixed fruits
6 cups pecans

Preheat the oven to 300 degrees.

Cream butter and sugar. Add 1 egg at a time and beat; add wine, milk, and rum extract, and beat well.

Sift the dry ingredients (except for ½ cup of the flour) and add to the wet ingredients.

Sprinkle fruits and pecans with ½ cup flour, and add them to the mixture.

Drop by spoonfuls on a greased cookie sheet.

Bake in the preheated oven for 15-20 minutes. *Makes 200 cookies.*

May be stored in freezer in plastic freezer containers.

SWEET-TOOTH DESSERT

1 small can crushed or chunk
  pineapple, drained
1 small can mandarin oranges,
  drained

1 large can cherry-pie filling
1 14-oz. can sweetened condensed milk
1 9-oz. container Cool Whip

Mix, mix, mix. Keep cool, cool, cool. Top with the Cool Whip.
Serves 6-8.

SWEET POTATO NUTTY CHEWIES

Wash and quarter three medium-sized sweet potatoes.
Boil until soft, peel, and mash to measure 3 cups.
Preheat the oven to 400 degrees.

3 medium-sized sweet
  potatoes (to equal 3 cups
  mashed)
2 cups sugar
5 tbsp. self-rising flour
½ cup milk

Dash salt
2 tsp. vanilla
1 cup nuts (preferably pecans)
1 cup coconut
½ stick butter

Add sugar, flour, and milk, and beat with electric mixer for 1
minute on medium speed. Add salt and vanilla.

With a spoon, fold in the nuts and coconut.

Melt the butter in a 9-by-13-inch pan with a depth of 2 inches. Add
the butter to the mixture, then pour it all back into the same pan.

Bake for 30 minutes in the preheated oven. Let cool. Cut into
squares to serve as a between-meal delight or as a dessert at meal-
time.

PRALINES

4 cups sugar	1 can water
4 tbsp. Karo syrup	1 tsp. butter
1 14-oz. can sweetened condensed milk	½ tsp. vanilla
	4-6 cups pecans

Mix sugar, Karo, condensed milk, and water thoroughly. Cook over a low fire until the soft-boil stage. Remove from heat.

Add butter, vanilla, and pecans. Beat until the mixture holds its shape.

Spoon onto buttered wax paper, and allow to cool.

RAISIN SUPREME À LA JUSTIN

6-8 cups seedless raisins	1 tsp. cinnamon
1 cup brandy	¼ tsp. bitters (Peychaud
1 cup Benedictine	or Angostura)
½ cup honey	

Put all of the ingredients in a pan on the stove and bring to a boil (not a rolling boil).

Simmer, covered, for 2 hours. Serve chilled.

"This delicious Supreme can be put over ice cream, lemon pie, or even vanilla wafers for a tasty treat."

LOUISIANA PRALINE, YAM, AND PECAN DESSERT CASSEROLE

4 medium Louisiana yams, cooked, peeled, and quartered (or 2 16-oz. cans)
2 eggs
½ cup firmly packed dark brown sugar
⅓ cup melted butter or margarine
1 tsp. salt
½ cup pecan halves

Preheat the oven to 350 degrees.

Mash yams in a large bowl. Beat in eggs, ¼ cup of the sugar, 2 tablespoons of the melted butter, and salt.

Turn into a 1-quart casserole dish. Arrange pecan halves on top, sprinkle with the remaining ¼ cup sugar, and drizzle with the remaining melted butter.

Bake, uncovered, in the preheated oven for 20 minutes. Serve warm with an orange sauce. *Serves 6.*

PUMPKIN-RAISIN LOAVES

BREAD

¾ can pumpkin
⅓ cup water
1 egg
1 tsp. pumpkin-pie spice

1 pkg. (14 oz.) apple-cinnamon
  muffin mix
½ cup raisins
Powdered Sugar Icing

Preheat the oven to 350 degrees.

Combine the pumpkin, water, egg, and pumpkin-pie spice in a large mixing bowl. Add the muffin mix and raisins; stir just until moistened.

Turn into three greased 5½-by-3-by-2-inch loaf pans (or one 9-by-5-by-3-inch loaf pan).

Bake small loaves in the preheated oven for 35-40 minutes. Bake larger loaf 50 minutes. Turn from the pan and cool on rack. *Makes 1 large loaf or 3 small ones.*

POWDERED SUGAR ICING

2 cups sifted powdered sugar   Milk

Add just enough milk to powdered sugar to give it a pouring consistency. Drizzle Powdered Sugar Icing over loaves.

SWEET POTATO SURPRISE CAKE

CAKE

1½ cups vegetable oil
2 cups sugar
4 eggs, separated
2½ cups sifted cake flour
3 tsp. baking powder
¼ tsp. salt
1 tsp. ground nutmeg

1 tsp. ground cinnamon
4 tbsp. hot water
1½ cups grated, raw sweet
  potatoes
1 cup chopped nuts
1 tsp. vanilla
Icing

Preheat the oven to 350 degrees.

Combine cooking oil and sugar; beat until smooth. Add egg yolks; beat well.

Sift the dry ingredients together. Add hot water to the liquid batter, then add the sifted dry ingredients.

Stir in the potatoes, nuts, and vanilla and beat well.

Beat the egg whites until stiff, and fold into the mixture.

Bake in three greased 8-inch layer cake pans in the preheated oven for 25-30 minutes. *Serves 10.*

ICING

1 box powdered sugar, sifted
1 8-oz. pkg. cream cheese

Milk with lemon juice or
  orange juice

Blend powdered sugar with the cream cheese.

Gradually add a small amount of milk to which lemon or orange juice has been added.

Use to ice Sweet Potato Surprise Cake.

Beer Birthday Cake

2 cups brown sugar
1 cup shortening
2 eggs
1 cup chopped nuts
2 cups chopped dates
1 tsp. cinnamon

½ tsp. allspice
½ tsp. ground cloves
3 cups sifted all-purpose flour
2 tsp. baking soda
½ tsp. salt
2 cups beer or ale

Preheat the oven to 350 degrees.

Cream the sugar and shortening. Stir in the eggs, nuts, dates, and spices.

In a separate bowl, sift together the flour, baking soda, and salt; stir in beer. Combine the beer mixture with the creamed mixture, and mix until well blended.

Bake in a large tube pan in the preheated oven for 1 hour and 15 minutes. If desired, ice with whipped cream or a caramel icing. *Serves 10.*

LOUISIANA'S CAJUN PEOPLE

The Cajuns were French colonists who settled in Nova Scotia in the early 1600s. They were farmers and trappers who made comfortable homes for their families and were happy in their new lives, although life in the wilderness was often hard. The Acadians were run out of Nova Scotia by the English in about 1755 because they would not swear allegiance to the king of England.

The Acadians (that's what they were called back then, since they lived in Acadia) were put on boats and sent away. Some settled along the East Coast of the United States, but many made their way to Louisiana, either by boat or on foot. It took many of them ten years or more to make the long trip from Nova Scotia. Families were broken up, and sweethearts were separated.

The first group of Acadians that reached Louisiana tried to land in New Orleans, but they had nothing, and people in New Orleans had very little, so they advised the Acadians to go up the Mississippi River to settle. That area had been settled by German families that John Law brought over as colonists. The Germans were kind enough to show the Acadians what plants were not poisonous and what game they could kill to eat. Later, the Acadians—now Cajuns— scattered throughout South Louisiana.

Index